Putting Analysis into Assessment

Undertaking assessments of need – a toolkit for practitioners

Ruth Dalzell and Emma Sawyer

national
children's
bureau

NCB promotes the voices, interests and well-being of all children and young people across every aspect of their lives.

As an umbrella body for the children's sector in England and Northern Ireland, we provide essential information on policy, research and best practice for our members and other partners.

NCB aims to:
- challenge disadvantage in childhood
- work with children and young people to ensure they are involved in all matters that affect their lives
- promote multidisciplinary cross-agency partnerships and good practice
- influence government policy through policy development and advocacy
- undertake high quality research and work from an evidence-based perspective
- disseminate information to all those working with children and young people, and to children and young people themselves.

NCB has adopted and works within the UN Convention on the Rights of the Child.

Published by the National Children's Bureau

National Children's Bureau, 8 Wakley Street, London EC1V 7QE
Tel: 020 7843 6000
Website: www.ncb.org.uk
Registered charity number: 258825

NCB works in partnership with Children in Scotland (www.childreninscotland.org.uk) and Children in Wales (www.childreninwales.org.uk).

ISBN 10: 1 904787 92 4
ISBN 13: 978 1 904787 92 1

British Library Cataloguing in Publication Data
A catalogue record for this book is available from the British Library

The views expressed in this book are those of the authors and not necessarily those of the National Children's Bureau.

Contents

Acknowledgements

The Putting analysis into assessment project was funded by Department for Education and Skills (DfES).

We would like to thank the managers and practitioners from the teams in Wandsworth and Leicestershire Children's Services departments for their participation in the project, and for sharing their ideas and experiences. Their feedback has informed the development of this toolkit.

Thanks also to Advisory Group members who gave generously of their time and expertise in the planning, development and undertaking of the project:

Julie Barnes, Independent Consultant
Jenny Gray, Professional Advisor, Children's Safeguards Policy Unit, DfES
Val Rogers, Sector Manager, Safeguarding and Commissioning, Wandsworth Social Services
Wendy Rose (Chair), Senior Research Fellow, The Open University
Jane Scannell, Service Manager, Children and Young People's Service, Leicestershire County Council
Dr. Janet Seden, Senior lecturer, Faculty of health and Social Care, The Open University
Jane Wiffin, Freelance Trainer and Senior Lecturer, PQCCA University of Bedfordshire
Laura Williams, Social Work Manager, Wandsworth Social Services (Children and Families Division)

We would also like to thank the following speakers at regional events and seminars relating to the project; Eileen Munro (London School of Economics), Jan Horwath (University of Leicester), Diana Bourn, (University of Leicester), Steve Walker (Royal Holloway, University of London), Moraene Roberts (ATD Fourth World) and Danielle Turney (Open University)

And thanks also to the practitioners and managers who attended the training courses that were developed following the project, and gave us feedback relating to the tools in this toolkit.

Finally, we would like to thank colleagues at NCB who provided input, ideas and support with the project and with this publication; Diane Hart, Joanna McCann, Alison Williams, Jane Powell, Sheryl Burton, Kate Thomas and Stephen Howell.

Dedication

The National Children's Bureau and Leicestershire County Council would like to acknowledge the contribution of Anne Brown, Children's Planning Officer, Leicestershire Social Services, whose enthusiasm and vision for this project was instrumental in its success. This publication is dedicated to her memory.

Foreword

The government's guidance, the *Framework for the Assessment of Children in Need and their Families,* emphasises the importance of analysing information after it has been gathered during an assessment of a child in need, and then arriving at judgements and making decisions about how best to help the child and family, and what needs to happen next. The analysis of often large quantities of personal information about children and families is a highly skilled task. It requires both knowledge and expert practice.

Social workers, with the support of their managers, have to consider the child's needs based on knowledge of what is expected of this particular child's development. They also have to consider the parents' capacity to meet their child's needs, drawing on knowledge about what would be reasonable to expect of parental care to a similar child. Equally important is consideration of family and environmental factors, often underestimated in making sense of a family's circumstances, drawing on knowledge about the impact these factors will have directly on a child's development and on parenting capacity.

The Department for Education and Skills commissioned Putting Analysis into Assessment to support social workers and their managers when they are assessing children in need and their families. The materials are designed to be used within teams and organisations to assist staff to develop and hone their analytical skills, which in turn will lead to improved judgements and decision-making.

Evidence from the two Local Authorities that piloted the materials is that staff both enjoyed using them and found them to be a valuable resource. I hope this experience is replicated in all local authorities and that their use will contribute to improving outcomes for children.

Jenny Gray
Professional Adviser, Children's Safeguards Policy Unit,
Department of Education and Skills

Introduction

Who is the toolkit for?

This toolkit has been written with the needs of social work practitioners and managers in mind, but it will also be useful to other professionals who are involved in assessing the needs of children and families. It is a practical resource, intended to provide tools and ideas to enhance analytical thinking by those undertaking assessments.

How can it be used?

A range of materials are provided within the book that are designed to: aid practitioners in their thinking before, during and at the conclusion of their work with children and families; provide managers with materials that can be used in supervision and practice development activities within the team; and provide trainers with suggested material and programmes for delivering training to those involved in social work and inter-agency assessments.

The book can be read from cover to cover or readers can go straight to sections and tools that are of interest or practical use in supporting their needs. Within each of the sections that contain resources and tools, there is a discussion about the tool's purpose, its relevance and possible uses, along with a case study and practice development session to demonstrate its use in practice.

The PowerPoint presentations (Presentations 1 to 7) accompanying this publication can be found in the appendix or can be downloaded from www.ncb.org.uk/resources/support. The presentations can be used in team-development or training courses.

What is in the toolkit?

The pack is divided into three main areas, the assessment in context, practical resources and moving forward.

Chapter 1 offers an introductory discussion about the importance of analysis within the social work task; the need to raise standards in this area; the relevant wider context in which social workers are operating; and describes the Putting analysis into assessment project, from which this toolkit has emerged.

Chapters 2, 3 and 4 outline resources and tools to help practitioners preparing for assessment, planning and conducting the assessment, making decisions and drawing conclusions, and reporting findings. Chapter 5 offers activities to assist with considering the culture of analysis within a team or agency. Chapter 6 provides training course materials and suggested programmes.

Chapter 7 considers the importance of team and agency culture further, discussing inter-agency issues and the opportunities and challenges there are for developing a more evidence-based and analytical approach within the social work task. It includes discussion on related issues such as what aids and hinders practitioners in being analytical; and what teams and agencies can do to support analytical practice. It also covers some discussion of wider issues, such as the interaction between social services and the court system; the impact of societal expectations on social workers; and the realities of trying to undertake complex, reflective work in the context of time and resource pressures.

1. The assessment process in context

Background

The Framework for the Assessment of Children in Need and their Families (Department of Health and others 2000) was developed to assess the needs of children under the Children Act 1989. It provides a systematic way of analysing, understanding and recording what is happening to children and young people, both within their families and in the wider context of the community in which they live, in order to be able to make professional judgements. These judgements include: whether the child is in need, or is suffering significant harm; what actions should be taken; and what services would best meet the needs of the particular child and family.

The Assessment Framework was intended to ensure that referral and assessment processes discriminate effectively between different types and levels of need; there is a timely service response to identified needs; and, in turn, better outcomes for children.

Although the intentions of the Children Act 1989 were to identify children in need and provide services to meet their needs, research studies – commissioned by the Department of Health (DH) and summarised in *Child Protection: Messages from research* (1995) – showed that child protection concerns continued to be the main trigger by which families gained access to services. In many authorities, it was only when there was evidence of potential significant harm to a child that access to family support services could be gained. This was the direct opposite of the intentions of Part 3 of the Act. The absence of a consistent approach nationally to the assessment of children in need meant that similar children were being treated very differently in different authorities.

The Framework for the Assessment of Children in Need and their Families takes the broad approach to identifying children in need, as intended by the Children Act 1989 and is designed to be used as a working tool for social workers and others involved in inter-agency assessments. The triangle of the assessment framework with its three domains: the child's developmental needs; the capacity of parents to meet those needs; and the impact of family, community and environmental factors, is now widely accepted across the range of agencies. There is no doubt that the assessment framework has improved and standardised practice across England. However, recent messages from inspections and research and, specifically, Cleaver and Walker (2004b) research into the implementation of the framework, have identified that analysis continues to be a major area of concern for practice.

The following comment from *Safeguarding Children: The joint chief inspectors report on arrangements to safeguard children* by the Department of Health and others (2002) highlights the issues, as follows.

> Too few assessments demonstrated an engagement with the social history of the family, a reflection on the evidence, synthesis and analysis and a concluding assessment of need and risk of significant harm.

And the following quote, from the 12th Annual Report of the Chief Inspector of Social Services (Department of Health 2003), identifies the centrality of skilled social work practice to the task of assessment.

Time and again the role of skilled social worker, in supporting, befriending and analysing the family has been found to be critical to the outcome for the child.

Analysing information in a way that makes the process transparent and able to be explained to a broad audience is no easy task and is challenging for a range of professionals, not just social workers. This book focuses on analysis because it is such an essential and integral part of the social work task and is the process upon which decisions about children's welfare, within and after assessments, hinge.

Before considering some of the specific challenges of social work analysis, it is important to define what is meant by 'analysis' in this context. A definition is important because when a practitioner is gathering information, reviewing what they know and making a decision, it is difficult for them to identify what part of the process constitutes 'analysis'. It is hardly surprising then, that social work decisions often take some explaining and justifying to service users, other professionals and in courts. In truth, analysis occurs throughout the whole assessment process – it influences whether assessments are carried out in the first place; and the decisions, however small, about how to go about them, who to involve and what information to gather.

Dictionary definitions of the words *assessment* and *analysis* suggest that they should in theory be comfortable bedfellows. Assessment means to appraise, measure, estimate or give consideration to a situation, whilst analysis means to examine, study, and break down into simpler elements.

It should therefore follow that in order to carry out a proper assessment of any situation, a certain amount of analysis needs to be undertaken. When faced with a complex situation one usually gathers all the facts and gives them consideration, separately and in relation to one another. This might be done by breaking down the information into simpler elements or manageable chunks under headings, then weighing up the options.

For example, a parent choosing a school for their child might gather information about which schools are available within travelling distance of where they live. They would then find out what they could about each school, asking certain questions determined by their individual priorities: Is the school more geared towards the arts, sciences or sports? How does this match with their child's needs or indeed their aspirations for him or her? What is the academic record of the school and what is its record on pastoral care and extra curricular activities? Is it convenient for local bus routes or walking to school and what is their child's preference? Would their child be able to transfer with existing friends or make friends they could socialise with outside of school? And, perhaps these days: What are the school dinners like?

The parent would then analyse the information gathered, which would require a certain amount of weighting of the different options. Is an easy journey to school more important than the school record in sports for example? This would lead ultimately to the decision that, hopefully, was right for their child and for them.

As any parent who has been through this process knows, this is not a pain-free activity and it is hard. There are some gains and losses and some likely compromise in any decision that is made. In many human situations there are also too many variables to ever be certain that the decision made is the 'right' one. Many of the factors that will contribute to the experience that the child has at school will be outside the parent's control, so the parent can only ever hope to make the best choice out of a range of available options at that given time.

Important as the decision in the above example undoubtedly is, it may seem rather straightforward when compared with some of the practice judgements and decisions required by social workers trying to support children and families living in the most challenging circumstances. Deciding how to protect and promote good outcomes for children – when they are living, for example, with parents with mental health or substance misuse problems, helping parents with learning disabilities to understand the needs of their children or trying to assess the likelihood of significant harm occurring to a child living in poverty or in the context of occasional neglect – throw up huge challenges for workers trying to reach a balanced view in the knowledge that decisions that they make could have a massive and enduring impact on a child's future health, well-being and family relationships.

In much the same way that the parent choosing a school for their child may have to settle for a decision that seems the 'best option' given all that they know; social workers, when dealing with such complex and unpredictable variables, can only hope to draw conclusions that are the 'least likely to be wrong' (Holland 2004). They must strive to do all they can to ensure that decisions and recommendations are made with rigorous checks and balances to counteract their human tendencies (to be influenced by time pressures, anxiety, false optimism or negative judgements).

So what makes the desired standard of analytical practice so elusive and difficult to achieve? Well, as discussed earlier, the decisions to be made are by no means easy. The use of evidence from research and theoretical approaches can support the task, but how far can these be generalised to individual situations and how confident can busy practitioners be in their acquisition and application of knowledge from such sources? How much time is there to be reflective? As one social worker in the Putting analysis into assessment project commented:

> You don't tend to have a pen and paper to hand when you reflect, as it is more likely to occur when you are doing something else, such as driving or washing up!

In fact, can a form – even guidelines, checklists or complex equations – show us how to be analytical? To what extent is analysis an intuitive creative skill that you've either got or you haven't? Theories about human decision-making abound; and some of these have been explored in the context of social work decision-making specifically by, for example, Eileen Munro (2002), Sally Holland (2004), and Ann Hollows (2003). These complex arguments are not explored in great depth in this toolkit, but they have been drawn upon to identify practical approaches for helping social workers to make judgements. These approaches were tested, with social workers, as part of the Putting analysis into assessment project (described on page 6); and their experiences are shared in Chapters 2 and 3. Also covered are some of the factors identified by practitioners as having a bearing on the nature and quality of analysis in their assessments.

First, however, it is important to consider the context within which social workers are operating, so as to take it into account when examining the many influences on their thinking, decision-making and capacity to be analytical.

Wider context

Social work with children and families does not operate in a vacuum. Practice is influenced by a whole range of a social and cultural norms and traditions. Definitions of childhood and child abuse are socially constructed, varying over time, and approaches to social work practice have been subject to rather more influence from fashion than perhaps some other professions.

> Practitioners ... are working within a field of evolving knowledge and changing public attitudes and expectations. Often they can find themselves at the forefront of discovery without the support of established knowledge.
>
> Butler and Williamson (1994) p.10

The unprecedented attention given to improving public services by the current government has impacted perhaps more on services for children than in any other area. A number of programmes have attempted to improve the management of services: for example, Quality Protects (1998) and, more recently, Change for Children (2004). In fact, wider society has in recent years been revolutionised in the approach taken to customer services and quality assurance. Feedback forms accompany almost every service used or car tyre changed and one can't complete an evening class in upholstery without being asked if one's learning objectives have been met. All this frenetic activity is aimed at improving the service being offered. Cynics may say that these systems have more to do with being able to tick boxes to achieve a level of self-satisfaction than improving the service offered but it is fair to say that this culture has permeated society and is accompanied by a desire to put those at the receiving end of services in a more central position. Moreover, it has led to greater transparency of decision-making and a need for processes to be more open to scrutiny and examination.

The Framework for Assessment of Children in Need and their Families (Department of Health and others 2000) provided practitioners and their managers with a core set of underpinning theories and approaches to use when assessing children in need and their families. This is now being followed by the Common Assessment Framework, which is intended to ensure that there is a common understanding and coordination of action across agencies in response to children's unmet needs. The common thread in all of these initiatives, and indeed in the Children Act 2004, is an attempt to keep the child at the heart of all interventions concerning them; to meet children's needs in a holistic way; and a belief that for any intervention to be effective it needs to start early and be ecological in nature.

Whilst all these initiatives are borne out of genuine attempts to improve practice and outcomes for children, it could be argued that most social workers have striven for holistic and preventive practice that is carried out in coordination with other agencies for many years; and that these ideas are not so much new as a reframing or restructuring in policy wording of the same ideas. However one sees it, there is no doubt that whilst the rhetoric, expectations and potential models that surround the social work task remain the focus of constant debate, this, along with the fear and pressure generated by tragedies and public responses to them (which invariably spur such debates), can be seen as potentially undermining practitioners' confidence and their ability to focus on the task in hand.

It is of course not the intention of such initiatives to undermine practice; instead they are moves towards improved practice, which are largely positive and create important opportunities. If social workers and others who share responsibility for assessing and responding to the needs of vulnerable children and families are to be supported in doing so effectively, they need the systems within which they operate to enable this, which is the aim of all these initiatives. However, the simple but very real difficulties practitioners face in finding the time, space and resources to enable them to reflect on their work also have to be addressed – in ways that policy and initiatives are unlikely to achieve alone. The culture of the team or agency that practitioners work within, the expectations they have of each other and that their managers have of them, all need to allow priority to be given to practitioners taking time to think carefully and to record this thinking usefully.

Putting analysis into assessment project

In response to the identified need for improvement in analysis within social work assessments, the National Children's Bureau undertook a project funded by the Department for Education and Skills (DfES) called Putting analysis into assessment, which ran from 2003–5. The tools and approaches outlined in this pack were tested within the course of the project.

The project aimed to improve the assessment of children and families by working directly with social work practitioners and managers to enhance their skills in analysis and to help them understand the basis for their judgements, to encourage a focus on outcomes for children and to explore how professional confidence and knowledge might be improved.

The project worked in depth with two local authorities, in their children and families teams, and involved practitioners and managers in other areas through seminars and workshops at a regional and national level. During the course of the project, the following input was provided to the practitioners and managers involved.

- Practice development sessions were undertaken, with the social work teams focusing on a range of themes relevant to analysis. This included the introduction of tools aimed at assisting with the analytical process and providing opportunities for practitioners to test out and appraise these tools.

- Individual interviews were offered to practitioners to discuss case decision-making in depth in a reflective way – looking back on what had influenced the life of a case and the decisions made along the way.

- The provision of feedback to practitioners, about the quality of analysis and balance within assessment reports, was drawn from an audit of case files.

- The teams' contributions to wider discussions about what aids and hinders analysis were facilitated by means of questionnaires, discussion and feedback forms.

- Team members attended seminars that took place in London and Leicestershire at which several high profile speakers, including Eileen Munro from London School of Economics, Jan Horwath from the University of Sheffield and Steve Walker from Royal Holloway, University of London, made presentations.

Four social work teams within two contrasting 'three star' local authorities were involved in the project.

One authority was a London borough, highly urban and widely diverse in ethnic and economic terms. The participating practitioners and managers were drawn from two Children in Need teams covering different geographical parts of the borough. Both teams were involved in undertaking assessments within the Assessment Framework, presenting cases at child protection conferences and undertaking court proceedings.

The other authority, in contrast, has a much more stable workforce. It is a county council in middle England and the teams selected serve a medium-sized, fairly affluent university town with relatively low unemployment and a less ethnically and culturally diverse population. The teams from this council were both involved in assessments of need for children and families, but with slightly different remits. One was a short-term team and dealt with initial assessments primarily (and some core assessments); and the other dealt with core assessments and longer-term intervention.

The London Borough was experiencing difficulty in recruiting and retaining permanent staff. This was demonstrated throughout the life of the project as around half of the practitioners no longer worked in the team by the end of the project and different staff were in their place. The other authority had a much more stable workforce.

As involvement in the project meant that the teams would be devoting a fair amount of time to taking part in practice development activities, it was important to establish, early on, what their own priorities and concerns were regarding their ability to be analytical within assessment. Managers and practitioner's views on the culture of analysis within their team were sought by interview and questionnaire (see page 113).

These activities provided information that helped shape the input to teams within the project. Managers, for example, told us in initial interviews that some staff lacked confidence around core assessments and there was a need and desire to move beyond information collection to greater analysis.

One manager commented that assessments were often seen by practitioners as a tool for obtaining resources and that, other than this, they were often completed for child protection conferences, which similarly had the potential to impact on the focus of the report. There were also comments that it was difficult to remain needs-led in the face of limited resources and that there can be a tension between quality and targets.

In the London borough, a high turnover of staff and a reliance on locums made consistency of practice difficult and tied up resources.

Managers and practitioners in both authorities mentioned, at the outset, the impact on their practice and priorities of the Laming Inquiry report into the death of Victoria Climbié (2003) in terms of seeking to implement its recommendations.

In both areas, managers said the direct use of research findings or exploration of evidence base was rarely apparent in assessments and their use of the *Assessment Framework: Family pack of questionnaires and scales* (Department of Health, Cox and Bentovim, 2000) was rare and patchy.

Summary of practice issues affecting analysis

Through the questionnaire, audits and less formal discussions with workers during practice development workshops, the following issues were identified as being of specific relevance to the question of analysis within assessments.

1. Most viewed the Assessment framework forms as leading them towards a holistic assessment.

2. Some types of cases, most notably parental mental health, parental substance misuse and children beyond parental control, were highlighted as particularly difficult areas for many practitioners when it comes to analysing the information collected.

3. There was lots of evidence in both authorities of thorough consultation with other relevant professionals involved with the families during the assessment process, although the implementation of the Assessment framework had *not*, in the opinion of most of the practitioners, encouraged a greater level of meaningful input from other professionals into the assessment process. Whilst the format was seen as encouraging a 'comprehensive trawl' of other people's views, many did not think most professionals involved with the family willingly took an active role in the assessment process.

4. When it comes to decision-making, the majority of practitioners described themselves as 'well supported' and said that their decisions were challenged in a supportive way. Supervision provided the opportunity for most to reflect, as did informal discussions with peers. However only a minority of participants in both authorities thought there was adequate time and space in team meetings to reflect on and discuss decisions made in assessments; and they would have liked more opportunity for this.

5. Practitioners were invited to explore the types of formal knowledge they drew on to assist in their analysis. The majority drew on theories and research relating specifically to child welfare (for example, attachment, child development, and ecological theories) at

least 'occasionally' if not 'a lot'. They also drew on government policy and guidelines 'a lot' or 'sometimes'.

6. However, whilst there was clearly a broad range of knowledge, most practitioners said they would *not* usually make explicit reference to theories when recording their assessments and this was also seen in the audits. Various reasons were given for this, including: lack of confidence about how sound or up to date their knowledge of a particular theory or piece of research is; and a fear that the use of research or theory may be 'used against' the social worker in the court arena, where their knowledge may be questioned or undermined with the use of 'experts' in an adversarial way.

7. Many participants felt that there were sufficient opportunities through training and development for accessing knowledge that would assist them in analysis and decision-making. However there were also comments that sometimes training was pitched too low, with fairly basic general courses over a range of subjects, and some would have liked to have been able to access more long-term, in-depth courses.

8. The majority of practitioners thought assessments were truly needs-led only 'sometimes' and identified the following factors as barriers: lack of time (generally as well as time limits of assessments); families withholding information; and difficulties in getting information from other agencies. Additionally, some practitioners thought that at times their high level of awareness about service/resource limitations led them to become unwittingly service-led in their assessments.

9. The audits yielded information on how clearly children's needs were identified. In some of the reports children's needs were not very clearly identified and, where they were, some areas of need were not covered; for example, identity and 'cultural' issues were mentioned in many assessments but rarely explored. However, audits carried out at a later stage of the project found identification of needs to be generally quite good. Approaches used in some reports, such as using chronological backgrounds breaking down and summarising needs, increased clarity.

10. The views of the child or young person were described either through what they had said or their presenting behaviour. At least half of the reports would have benefited from some further discussion regarding to what extent the child's views had been elicited so far. It was often not clear from reports how much contact the social worker had had with the child and in what contexts; that is, had they seen the child without their parents as well as with them? More often than not, the parents' views became the focus of what was written.

It was clear from the practitioners involved in the project that on the whole they were committed to making sound, balanced and sufficiently analytical decisions and that they recognised that in order to do so, all information needs to be considered and weighed and that it is necessary to actively seek out alternative points of view or information. They were generally good at consulting with other professionals, although met barriers sometimes and found that despite good intentions, it is hard to maintain a focus that is truly needs-led.

All participants felt there was room for increasing their knowledge and confidence in order to improve their analytical skills, but that lack of time, volume of work and the challenging nature of the work make it difficult to be analytical and reflective – both of which are essential to good decision-making.

However, through being involved in the project and being introduced to tools and ideas – to assist them in thinking about cases, decisions and their ability to analyse – participants in the main felt they had benefited in terms of their confidence and capacity to be analytical. The reflection required and discussion time allowed during the project was itself a key factor in this.

2. Preparing for assessments

The activities in this chapter are to assist practitioners in becoming more analytical before and during the planning and preparation stages of assessments, although the materials themselves could be used at any stage in the assessment process.

Preparing oneself: The reflective mindset

This section looks at the importance of developing a critical and reflective mindset and examines some of the arguments about how people think and make decisions. It looks at the importance of emotion in decision-making; and introduces a practice tool designed to help practitioners understand the influences on their own decision-making.

Reflective mindset

Analysis not only happens at the end of the assessment. It could be argued that, in addition to happening throughout the assessment process, it needs to start before the case is even referred. Applying a more analytical approach to assessment requires the practitioner to have already begun developing a critical and reflective mindset; and so be ready to approach the task in an attentive manner.

Reder and Duncan (1999) refer to this as the development of a *dialectic* mindset. This concept has been around since the teachings of Socrates and follows the principles of promoting 'the acquisition of knowledge through dialogue and argument'. This idea has much in common with the concept of reflective practice. Moon (1999) describes reflective practice as follows.

> A set of abilities and skills to indicate the taking of a critical stance, an orientation to problem solving or state of mind.

Schön contributed significantly to the notion of *reflecting on experience* to improve action in professional practice; firstly, through work on learning organisations and latterly, through his work on the reflective practitioner (Schön 1983) and the notion of reflection-in-action or, put more simply, 'thinking on our feet'. This involves looking to our experiences, connecting with our feelings and attending to the theories in use. It entails building new understandings to inform our actions in the situation that is unfolding.

Holland (2004) refers to *reflection*, which she describes as 'critical thoughtfulness' about practice experience before, during and after practice events. She also introduces the more complex notion of *reflexivity*, which she describes as a 'fundamental examination of the discourses and knowledge systems that underpin interactions in social, care'. Reflective or even reflexive practice is an aspiration for most social workers but may seem a somewhat esoteric goal in the cut and thrust of team life. In reality, it is something that needs to be supported on a variety of different levels; individual, team and agency, and which requires careful nurturing and the time and space to thrive.

Practitioners and team managers gave feedback, during the Putting analysis into assessment project, that the impact upon people's ability to be more thoughtful and reflective was one of the most significant benefits of the practice development work in teams. It seems to have been the introduction of the notion of thinking more critically or thinking about how we think, combined with the space created for the team to reflect together at the same time that brought about this change. The following comments, made by practitioners during the project evaluation, support this.

> The project has affected assessments, evaluations and reasons for decisions are more confident/thought through.

> As a team we discuss more cases/practice share ideas, examine existing assessments more thoroughly, the team has benefited from spending project sessions together.

> We appreciated time away from casework responsibilities for personal development to benefit case work.

The project created an opportunity for individual practitioners to reflect on the influences on their own practice and on decisions that had been made, in a safe and supportive way within the team. Being able to do this, over a period of time with an external facilitator, contributed to the development of a habit of doing this within supervision and peer discussion – a habit that was still apparent several months after the fieldwork had been completed. This could be described as a kind of 'priming', which is akin to 'learning to learn' as described by Caxton (1999).

Intuition and analysis

One area that the Putting analysis into assessment project concentrated on was understanding the balance between intuition and analysis in effective decision-making within social work.

Intuitive thinking tends to be the way in which most people operate innately. O'Sullivan (1999) suggests that although intuition is often seen as an important aspect of professional decision-making, its definition and nature are problematic. O'Sullivan points out that the absence of deliberation in intuitive decision-making means that it is a relatively quick way of making use of limited information by sensing patterns and filling in gaps. He suggests that professional intuition is something that develops through experience and cannot be formally taught.

Munro (2002) discusses the analytical–intuitive divide in social work and relates this to the broader debates contained in theories of decision-making over the centuries. She explores the strengths and weaknesses of both approaches: highlighting the fact that intuitive thinking is a largely unconscious process which is key to the way people make sense of the world; being swift, simple and drawing on imagination, empathy, gut feelings and past experience. She also makes the point that it is often an unreliable approach, which is flawed as a source of public knowledge as it is difficult to articulate, prone to bias, relies on narrow samples and is limited by personal experience.

In contrast to this, analytical thinking is a 'step by step, conscious, logically defensible process' (Hammond 1996), which is focused on breaking decisions down into elements, which are then carefully considered in relation to each other.

Analysis, according to Munro (2002), is based on empirical research and a much wider knowledge base that has been tested and is open to public scrutiny. Many aspects of a subject have been studied and, due to the wide availability of research databases nowadays, comprehensive overviews of research studies are available. Munro sounds a note of caution with regard to analytical and actuarial[1] approaches and states that, in some areas, there is

---

1 A mathematical or statistical approach based on interpretations drawn from risk analysis schedules or checklists.

still a limited knowledge base; that findings are often only tentative at best; and that trying to apply research findings across populations can be dangerous. Findings cannot be viewed uncritically – human judgement is still a critically important element.

Research by Dreyfus and Dreyfus (1986, referred to in Munro 2002 p.26) found that, in practice, clinicians begin by relying heavily on the analytical actuarial tools and then, over time, gradually integrate these into their thinking so that they are eventually drawing on them unconsciously. She points out that this is somewhat different in the case of social work, as social workers often start out by drawing on a lot of folk psychology. She makes the following point.

> Child protection workers need to become more analytical and critical to improve accuracy – make reasoning more open and accountable. The centrality of empathy and intuition needs to be acknowledged but practice can be improved by developing professionals' analytical skills.

O'Sullivan (1999) likewise suggests that social workers need to know how to go about analysis whilst at the same time developing their intuitive expertise, as both intuition and analysis have an important role in social work.

Jones and others (2006) discuss the importance of applying an evidence base thoughtfully and critically; and the limitations of trying to apply it in a precise or numerical way due to the complexity of the interaction of factors in human situations . The evidence base in question is one comprising factors associated with future harm in situations where a child has previously suffered harm. They stress that the process of decision-making needs to be as open as possible from an ethical as well as a practical point of view. Openness requires careful thought by the practitioner, and encourages reflection on personal responses; an evaluation of the importance of data; and allows for scrutiny by supervisors and other stakeholders.

Emotions

The place of emotions in decision-making and particularly in relation to social work must not be overlooked. It has long been recognised that developing emotional intelligence and being alert to one's own emotional responses and what they might mean in the context of interactions with children and families, is essential to effective practice. That great teacher of social work, Clare Winnicot, wrote powerfully in 1977 about the impact of emotions on social work with children.

> Whenever a social worker intervenes in the life of a family which includes a child or children there is a story behind the intervention, and the social worker needs to know that story and its effect on each child, and to live through the experience with the child as fully as possible, without denying the pain, and accepting the sadness, anger and depression that the situation gives rise to. In this way, moments of great pain can become moments of truth on which a future might be built.

Winnicott (1977) also pointed out the need for awareness within social work departments of the support needed for social workers dealing with emotionally demanding situations, when she wrote:

> Social service departments need to allow for this strain on their social work staff, to understand it, and to devise ways of meeting it within the structure and organisation of the department.

What Winnicott is highlighting is the potential of emotion to help a practitioner's understanding of a situation. For example, a social worker faced for the first time with the expression of grief by a seven-year-old girl at being returned to foster carers at the end of a contact visit with her mother, will need to balance the natural human response of wanting to comfort the child and stem the expression of grief, with the benefits to the child of being able to express their feelings. Working with the child's feelings, rather than against them, is likely to help the worker build their own understanding of the child's inner world and the family relationships and circumstances.

A practitioner who is practised at understanding their own emotional responses will recognise that when they feel depressed or helpless after interviewing a particular client this might give insight into what the client is feeling or experiencing.

O'Sullivan (1999) points out that a wide range of emotions are experienced in social work – fear, anxiety, hope, compassion – and that social workers have to cope with their own emotions and those of the clients and other stakeholders.

A model for understanding the nature of expertise

In her book *Effective Child Protection* (2002), Munro introduces a model (see page 15) to aid understanding of the nature of expertise, or in other words, categories of knowledge and skills that come into play when social workers are making judgements and decisions.

Munro's model was introduced to practitioners during the Putting analysis into assessment project and assisted them in reflecting on their decisions and, in so doing, to become attuned to the usefulness of unpicking and reflecting on decisions and judgements. This was part of the process of developing a critical and reflective mindset.

The model was described to practitioners as being a bit like listening to an orchestra or a band playing. You can either, simply listen and enjoy the music; or you can try and listen for particular instruments and appreciate the role they are playing in the overall sound. Once you have started to do this it tends to stay with you as a way of listening. The practitioners found Munro's 'Pie chart' model helpful as it made them more conscious of the formal knowledge they were drawing on; the critical skills they were using; and how factors such as emotions and experience were coming into play.

PRACTICE TOOL: A PIE CHART OF KNOWLEDGE AND SKILLS

Munro's model

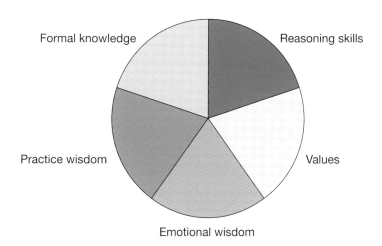

Values: all practice takes place in an ethical framework including, for example, consideration of the balance of rights and needs and awareness of discrimination in all its forms.

Reasoning skills: ability to reflect critically on one's practice; and reason, from a basis of experience and knowledge. Ability to understand the balance between intuition and analysis in one's own decisions; and the ability to make a conscious appraisal of risks and benefits flowing from actions.

Emotional wisdom: Awareness of the emotional impact of the work on oneself and others and the ability to deal with this and use it as a source of understanding about behaviour of children, families, self and other professionals.

Practice wisdom: folk psychology, social norms, cultural diversity; a combination of everyday skills and wisdom with enriched skills drawn from training and practice experience.

Formal knowledge: Law, policies and procedures and theories; empirical research evidence drawn, for example, from training and reading.

The above model is reproduced and adapted from Munro, E (2002) 'Categories of knowledge and skills', p.12, Figure 2.1.

CASE STUDY 2.1

Ellen is on duty in an office in a Midlands town. A referral comes in from the local general hospital antenatal department. Adanna, a 32-year-old Nigerian woman has walked into the accident and emergency department apparently in the early stages of labour. She has not attended any antenatal appointments and is not known to the hospital. She has a three-year-old child with her, a little girl called Ifeoma. Adanna has told the A&E doctors that she is HIV positive but that she does not know if her child Ifeoma is. Adanna is also very poorly with pre-enclampsia, a condition associated with high blood pressure in later pregnancy.

She has given her address as a hotel on Ellen's patch and states that she has lived in the area for three weeks, having moved from London where she had lived with her boyfriend for 18 months. She states that she came to this country two years ago from Nigeria but is unable to say anything about her current status.

The child, Ifeoma, seems well dressed and well fed. Adanna has named her sister as her next of kin and given an address in West London for her.

The hospital are asking Social Services to make arrangements to care for Ifeoma in the short term. Staff also state that there may be other decisions to be made once the baby is born, depending on the outcomes of the tests and how unwell Adanna is.

Ellen will be drawing on knowledge, skills and values drawn from different sections of the pie chart in deciding what actions to take and how to work with this situation.

Formal knowledge will be required because she needs to know the legal framework that sets out the local authority's responsibilities for Ifeoma. She will know that there is a requirement to work in partnership wherever possible with Adanna and enable her to bring up her own child. She will also know that she has to undertake checks with Health and Education and other agencies to find out any relevant information, and that these agencies have a duty to cooperate under Part V of the Children Act 1989. She will have to make a decision whether to receive Ifeoma into care under Section 20 of the Children Act 1989, or indeed whether Ifeoma could be placed with Adanna's sister and receive support as a Child in Need under Section 17 of the 1989 Act. Formal knowledge about child development theory and attachment theory will also affect the decision about where to place Ifeoma. Knowledge of local procedures will determine how Ellen consults with her managers in making the decision. Ellen will also need formal knowledge of asylum and immigration policy and procedures, or will need to take advice from someone who has this knowledge.

Practice wisdom may come into play as Ellen draws on her own past experience of placing children with local foster carers. Her knowledge of the skills and attitudes of local carers may well impact upon the decision. Her knowledge of the likely attitudes and practices within the local hospital will also come into play. Ellen has worked with a number of mothers who are HIV positive, is part of a network of practitioners who work in this area and has undergone a significant amount of training. Ellen's past experience with a similar case, was that, when the Home Office were contacted for information the mother in question went underground. This means that Ellen will wait until she has been able to build some trust with Adanna before taking these steps again.

Emotional wisdom features, as Ellen is able to predict the possible range of Ifeoma's emotional reactions to separation from her mother and is able to discuss with foster carers the meaning of her responses and behaviour. Ellen is herself pregnant and is aware that this particular referral will stir up feelings in her that will possibly be heightened by her experience of pregnancy. Emotional wisdom will also determine the level to which she is able to engage with Ifeoma and her mother.

Values will come into play. Ellen adheres strongly to values about working in partnership, so will do all she can to involve Adanna in the decisions made about Ifeoma and will keep her informed about her progress. She will be aiming to get Ifeoma reunited with Adanna as soon as Adanna is well enough to care for her. She will also work with sensitivity to the cultural differences between herself and Adanna; and Adanna's experiences of living in a society where the dominant culture is different to her own. She feels strongly that parents and children affected by HIV have a right to confidentiality and to retain control over how their medical and social needs are met.

Reasoning skills will come into play when Ellen reflects on how her own assumptions and those of the medical staff – and indeed Adanna and Ifeoma – are affecting their responses to one another and their expectations. Reasoning skills will also operate when Ellen thinks through the consequences of decisions that are going to need to be taken; such as where to place Ifeoma and how to manage contact.

Practice development session 1

The nature of expertise

This session can either be done with a whole team during a team meeting or as part of a longer training course.

Aim

To encourage practitioners to reflect on the range of skills, knowledge and experience that they draw on in practice and to apply this understanding to practice.

Method

a) Begin by asking the group what they understand by the word **expertise**. Allow everyone in the group to contribute by means of an **ideas storm**. Write down everything that is said, on a whiteboard or flip chart, without questioning it.

b) Generate a discussion about who it is that participants feel have expertise in children and families work; and how different people within the system view it. If necessary, prompt them asking questions such as: Who do parents/teachers/magistrates/social workers/children tend to view as experts? Why?

c) Give a presentation on the nature of expertise; the dichotomy between thinkers (analytical and intuitive); and the importance of both analytical and intuitive thinking over the years using the relevant slides from Presentation 1. See Appendix or download from www.ncb.org.uk/resources/support. Stop after the 'Exercise' slide.

d) Ask participants to generate a list of the strengths and weaknesses of analytical and intuitive approaches. Then resume the slide show, which will provide feedback on their list.

e) Introduce the slide of the pie chart and explain the range of knowledge, skills and so on that a practitioner might be using when making a decision.

f) Invite the participants to form pairs. Distribute Munro's model (page 15), one to each pair. You may also want to give them case study 2.1, which illustrates the model used within a case.

g) Ask participants, in their pairs, to reflect on their practice over the past couple of months and think about how they have drawn on the various sections of the pie chart. If necessary, prompt them by asking: Do you tend to rely on one part of the pie chart or does it vary depending on the type of case? What external factors impact on how you draw on the sections of the pie chart? Has reflecting on this led you to think that you need to change the way in which you draw on the sections of the pie chart? If so, is there anything you can do about this?

h) Reconvene the full group. Invite feedback on the key points from the discussion. If necessary, prompt them by asking: Did this help you to think about the knowledge, skills and experience you are drawing on in your practice? Has it highlighted any of your strengths or weaknesses? Does it have any implications for your individual practice or team's practice? Are there any actions you can use to strengthen your practice, based on the issues that have been highlighted today?

i)   **Alternatively (or in addition)** ask participants to think through one particular case, remembering key decisions that were made and deciding which elements of the pie chart came into play – this activity to be done as individuals, followed either by discussion in pairs or a general feedback session in the full group. One person could be asked to talk through their case and describe how the different elements were drawn upon at different times. (For further details of this activity, see The Critical Decision method on page 95.)

Cultural review

This section introduces the idea of applying approaches more usually used in social research to assist in the assessment situation. In particular we focus on the Cultural review, which is a method of examining cultural assumptions.

In her book *Child and Family Assessment in Social Work Practice* (2004), Holland explores the importance of the impact of the social worker on the assessment relationship and introduces the notion of the reflective and reflexive practitioner. She describes reflexivity as follows.

> A circular process of thought and action, with our thoughts and beliefs interacting with and affecting service users, and their responses and experiences in turn affecting our thoughts and belief systems .

Holland refers to the need to be critically aware of the impact of ourselves and our belief systems on the assessment; and of the service users response to this. She suggests that this will include 'categories' associated with ourselves, such as gender, race and professional status; our agency culture; and dominant theories, practices and assumptions within our occupation. She highlights the need to address these issues in supervision and also, if appropriate, with service users.

She explores some of the literature (Anderson 1990, Farmer and Owen 1995) that looks at the importance of being sensitive to the impact of issues, such as gender and ethnicity, on the allocation of cases.

This is also an area that was explored in Holland's own research, *The Coastal Cities Study* (Holland 2004). In her study, social workers were invited to reflect upon their own contribution to the assessment relationship. They identified some of the difficulties involved, such as power differentials on the grounds of class, race and gender; and were also invited to examine the compensatory tactics they used to minimise the effects of these potential barriers in practice. One social worker interviewed on the study stated the following.

> I am very much aware that I am a mixed race man and she is a white woman, I think we have some common ground in the fact that we both have small children and I can disclose things about my children and so on ... I think in a sense the issues of class relate to the fact that I am employed, in full-time employment and she isn't, so I mean there's an imbalance there.

The worker concerned was able to highlight some of the imbalances in the relationship between himself and a client and some of the practices he had used to minimise these.

Holland makes the case for applying methods more usually applied by social researchers – in gathering, organising and analysing data – to the social work task of assessment. Several of her suggestions have been incorporated into this toolkit, including her thoughts on hypothesising and on organising data in reports.

One method introduced in Holland's book (2004), which was originally suggested by McCracken (1988) and featured in Shaw (1997), is called a 'cultural review'.

This is a method for systematically looking at all our cultural categories in relation to the subject at hand. Ideally, it is suggested, this should be carried out at an early stage in the assessment. The purpose of undertaking the cultural review is for the practitioner to alert themselves to areas where their own assumptions, prejudices or simply lack of knowledge might have a bearing on their response to a family and, ultimately, on the approach taken to working with them. Similarly, issues that a worker may be carrying in their head, such as agency norms and awareness, will also have an impact; as will the families' likely assumptions about the worker and the agency.

Perhaps the most appropriate point to undertake a cultural review, time permitting, would be *before* the first interview or contact with a family after a referral has been received.

The review consists of a series of trigger questions. It is possible to do it as a detailed exercise taking from 20–40 minutes; or else, as is much more likely to be practicable, practitioners should, with a bit of practice, be able to hold the questions in their head and address them mentally before a first meeting and then reflect upon the process afterwards.

This model was introduced to practitioners on the Putting analysis into assessment project. The feedback received was that social workers were surprised by some of the answers generated by the exercise. Most of them found it very useful and felt that they would be likely to use it again in practice. One worker commented that it assisted with analysing information, arguing for resources and explaining a decision to a colleague. She also said that:

> Particular needs/requirements were highlighted as were differing world views and methods of interpreting events and conducting life tasks.

This model is applicable to developing a more analytical approach to assessment in that it reveals at an early stage some of the unconscious processes and hidden influences on a practitioner's ability to engage with families. This process is referred to by McCracken (1988, p.33) in Holland (2004, p.130) as 'familiarisation and defamiliarisation', which means that by bringing assumptions and underlying influences on our thinking into awareness we can stand apart from them and see them more objectively and, if necessary, take compensatory action. In Case study 2.2, we have shown how two different cases could generate answers in the cultural review. These are drawn from social workers' responses to the cultural review questions during the Putting analysis into assessment project.

Cultural review

- What do I know about individuals and families with this particular cultural background or life experience?

- Where does my knowledge come from?

- What prejudices may I hold (positive or negative)?

- What do I know/expect about children of this (these) age(s), their lives and needs?

- What might surprise me about this family and why would it be a surprise?

- How might this family/the parents/child/siblings/community perceive me?

- How might the assessment and my agency be perceived?

- What impact might the assessment have on the family's life and on their perception of their lives?

- What agency norms and practices do I take with me on an assessment? (For example, awareness of risk, thresholds of 'good enough parenting', resource restrictions.)

The cultural review questions above, based on McCracken's (1988) *Cultural Review* and featured in Shaw (1997), are based on Holland's (2004, p.130) use of the questions for social work assessment.

CASE STUDY 2.2

During the Putting analysis into assessment project, a number of groups of participants completed the cultural review exercise. Table 2.1 gives examples of the responses given by two different groups after being given very brief details of referrals.

Table 2.1

Cultural review questions	Responses from practitioners	
	Case details	Case details
	3-month-old baby of Somalian origin	**12- and 14-year-old White British girls**
	Referring agent: Police/immigration	*Referring agent:* School
	Reason for referral: 17-year-old minor/ asylum seeker with baby – unaccompanied	*Reason for referral:* Concerns re parental discipline, poor attendance, poor hygiene, parental mental health issues
	Family structure: No known family at present	*Family structure:* Mum (29 yrs), Dad (32 yrs), 14 yr old girl, 12 yr old girl, 3 yr old boy, 10 mth old twins, boy and girl
	Other agencies involved: Police, immigration, who have reference to NASS we assume	*Other agencies involved* School, HV, CPN, school nurse, Connexions, GP, NSPCC (anon. Refs), CPU
	Family previously known? Not to social services locally	*Family previously known?* Parents in care. Also previous sec 17 practical and financial help
	Length of time in area: 12 hours – presumed	*Length of time in area* 12 months (moved around Midlands)
	Other significant information: Baby sick/dehydrated and malnourished	*Other significant information:* Isolated and stigmatised in local community, don't take up support, housing issues, financial – don't manage well
What do I know about individuals and families with this particular cultural background or life experience?	Nothing/language/malnutrition– poverty childcare culture/'difficult to work with' (hearsay) large extended family at home	Early pregnancy, poor education, poor employment, low self-esteem/self-worth. MH problems. Attachment problems – also relate to their attachment to their children. Little family support. Distrust of agencies/dislike of SSD. Fear of childcare support. Aware of 'the system'
Where does my knowledge come from?	Media/other professionals/previous experience of asylum seekers/lack of knowledge = assumptions	Research/reading/ literature. Practice wisdom, knowledge, colleagues, personal experience, service users, training, and other agencies

Cultural review questions	Responses from practitioners	
	Case details	*Case details*
What prejudices may I hold (positive or negative)?	As above/presume needs resources and help and assume entrance is illegal	Failure to parent, history 'repeating itself'. As above, mostly negative
What do I know/expect about children of this (these) age(s), their lives and needs?	Good experience of child development – realistic expectations, very dependant, needs complete care Needs strong attachment to care giver	Time of change, identity quite well established in behaviour. Guarded and protective of family. May be young carers. Friends/peers important. May be rebellious. Emotional problems/ moody. Peer pressure. Expectations from school – academic pressure. Poor supervision at home. Need a lot of feeding. Self-image – fashion
What might surprise me about this family and why would it be a surprise?	If came in legally to meet up with family/if doesn't want support/if has financial support/if can speak English fluently/to meet up with wealthy family	Strengths and resilience can be challenging to professionals. Prejudices regarding passivity and 'client'
How might this family/the parents/child/siblings/ community, perceive me?	Official/threatening/powerful/take child?/judging	**Parents:** Threat, unrealistic, interfering, helpful, understanding, bit of a pushover **Children (12 & 14):** fearful – 'care', helpful, willing to listen to them, concerned, make it worse/better
How might the assessment and my agency be perceived?	As above	Unnecessary, interfering provider of services/goods/items, unpredictable, frightening
What impact might the assessment have on the family's life and on their perception of their lives?	Major – might have to return/undermine parenting/self-esteem/values	Might give some insight. Provide some resources, help with parenting, improve. Might have little effect
What agency norms and practices do I take with me on an assessment? (For example, awareness of risk, thresholds of 'good enough parenting', resource restrictions)	Financial resources/timescales/risk of significant harm/thresholds/ individual perceptions of agency's 'norms'/procedures and other agencies' procedures	ACPC – guidance and procedures on neglect. Thresholds for assessment. Lack of intensive family support resources locally. 'Heartsink' case – not much we can do – too entrenched

Practice development session 2

Cultural review

Aim

To demonstrate how undertaking a cultural review at the very beginning of a case creates opportunity for openness and reflection about influences on practice.

Method

a) Invite participants to form pairs and to ideas storm what they think are the things (assumptions, questions, expectations and baggage) that they might bring to an assessment before they even meet the family. Either ask them to write their ideas down on sticky notes or take feedback from the whole group and record it on a whiteboard or flip chart.

b) Reconvene the full group. Give information on cultural review and how it is used by social researchers to help them understand how their own prejudices and experiences might slant the way in which they approach a piece of research, so that they can actively take steps to counter this tendency. Use Presentation 2 (up to slide 6), or make presentation into a handout and talk through key points (see Appendix or download the presentation from www.ncb.org.uk/resources/support).

c) Divide participants into small groups and give them some very brief referral information on a case or on several different cases. (This could be taken from Case studies 2.1 and 2.2 or, if a whole team is present, use cases recently referred to the team.) Distribute the cultural review questionnaire (page 21) and ask the participants to consider the questions in their groups and note down all their responses, even if they vary. Encourage them to discuss and debate but stress that they do not need to reach a consensus.

d) Invite feedback from the group – this can be detailed if you have time or just a point from each group.

e) Reconvene the full group and ask participants if the activity raised any issues for them. Did they find it helpful? Would it be possible to do this before conducting an assessment? Could they take something useful from it into practice? If time would not allow them to do a full cultural review, could they do an abbreviated version or keep certain questions in their heads to think about whilst on their way to a visit?

It is likely that the exercise has made people think about the prejudices that they and families might hold; and about how cultural issues in wider society and in their own agencies will impact on the way in which they approach a first meeting with a family.

Hypothesising

This section introduces the notion of hypothesising. It looks at the origins and meaning of the word and how it should be considered to be a key feature of assessment practice. It goes on to examine how keeping an open mind and thoughtfully exploring different hypotheses assists in the assessment process and in explaining decisions that have been made.

The word *hypothesis* has its origins in ancient Greek and means 'a proposed explanation for a phenomenon' (Wikipedia – online dictionary). In modern day usage, a hypothesis is a provisional idea or explanation which has to be evaluated or tested. The idea needs to be either confirmed or disproved. The hypothesis should be 'falsifiable', which means it is possible for it to be shown to be false, usually by observation. Even if confirmed, the hypothesis is not necessarily proven, but remains provisional.

Hypothesising is a core activity within social work assessment. Holland (2004) states:

> The cornerstone of analysis in assessment work might be seen as the process of building hypotheses for understanding a family situation and developing these until they include a plan for the way forward.

This process of building, testing out and discarding hypotheses starts at the earliest point of contact. As soon as a referral is received into a social work team the practitioner will begin consciously or unconsciously to form some hypotheses of what is happening within the family.

For example, if a headteacher rings the duty team at 5pm to say that they are concerned about a seven-year-old girl who has not been collected from school that day (and who is often not collected on time, regularly arrives at school very late, is often brought by strangers, is usually dirty, unkempt and seemingly underfed), the duty officer is likely to be mentally hypothesising about what is happening within the family during the initial conversation. They may have several hypotheses that spring to mind immediately, of which the following are an example.

1. Parent has started working and has not been able to arrange proper childcare for child.

2. Parent or carer is depressed or ill and has become unable to meet the child's day-to-day needs.

3. Child is a scapegoat within the family and is therefore neglected or abused.

4. This is a chaotic family who only just cope at the best of times and some event has occurred to tip them into an unacceptable level of chaotic neglect.

5. The child's parents are misusing alcohol or other substances and are often too 'out of it' and unable to care properly for the child or bring her to school.

They would certainly check out some of their hypotheses during an initial conversation with the referrer and may even ditch one or more of them at this stage. The formation of various hypotheses and the decision taken about the steps needed to investigate the matter further will be influenced by a range of factors, for example: practice wisdom, personal values, and formal knowledge.

The practitioner is also likely to be susceptible to what Sheldon (1987) and Scott (1998) (cited in Holland 2004) refer to as 'our natural human tendency to be "verificationists"'. This means that we tend to form an explanation for a family's or individual's circumstances early on in our contact with them and then we tend to seek information that will confirm these original hypotheses.

Similarly, Munro's research (1999) into the findings of inquiries into child deaths highlights that a common error identified in inquiries was a 'failure to revise risk assessments' and that in numerous cases there was failure to check more widely or reappraise original judgements when new evidence arose.

Hollows (2003) refers to this tendency as 'unconflicted adherence', that is, where a new risk is discounted and the current strategy is maintained without change.

Raynes in Calder and others (2003) suggests that workers often remain narrowly focused on proving or disproving whether the original risk remains and fail to consider the broader picture. He suggests that practitioners should consider all the possibilities about what is happening and address each hypothesis, only discarding it when there is clear evidence to do so. In the Stepwise approach to assessment, as shown in the illustration below, the hypothesis stage first appears early in the process of assessment. Although one would argue that, as demonstrated earlier, the process of hypothesising starts earlier, that is, at the point of referral, this model is nevertheless helpful for giving a structured approach to the stages of the assessment process and the place of forming, testing out and discarding hypotheses within that process.

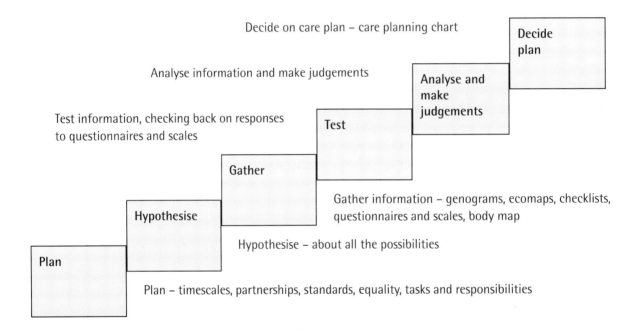

Illustration of hypothesis within the stepwise model of assessment

The above model is based on work by De Mello and Yuille and is adapted from Calder and Hackett (2003) *Assessment in Childcare: Using and developing frameworks for practice*, p.122, Figure 1 'A stepwise model for children and familiy assessments'.

The illustration above locates the various assessment activities at the specific stages of the stepwise model. Similarly, Margaret Adcock (2000) describes several overlapping phases of assessment and further explores the distinctions between analysis, judgements and decisions.

As identified earlier, the process of hypothesising might continue throughout the assessment process as long as new information continues to emerge. The information should be drawn from a range of sources using a variety of methods. In order to counter the verificationist tendency earlier identified, Holland (2004) argues as follows.

> We should always look for data, or information, that might disprove, or at least throw doubt on, our understanding. The reason for such an orientation is that it actively works against our human tendency to distort what we see in order to fit with our fixed explanations.

New information is sought with the specific purpose of increasing understanding about what is happening within the family and how this is impacting on the well-being of the child or children under consideration. It is vital to make the search wide-ranging and to do it in partnership with family members as much as possible. Using different strategies for gathering the information, rather than relying on one narrow method, is also important. Methods for gathering information may include the following.

1. Interviewing parents and children

2. Interviewing professionals who know the family

3. Employing direct observation and child observation

4. Using questionnaires and scales with family members

5. Using play or drawing and creative approaches to communicating with children

6. Making reference to research or theory

Testing and evaluating hypotheses is a key part of the process. The timescales ascribed to different levels of assessment (initial and core) will limit the depth of exploration that can be undertaken but, even in an initial assessment, it is possible and indeed expected to generate possible hypotheses and explore these. Indeed, noting that some important hypotheses have not been tested during an initial assessment may well indicate that a core assessment is necessary in order to undertake further enquiries.

PRACTICE TOOL: QUESTIONS TO ASSIST IN HYPOTHESISING

Questions for hypothesising and reviewing hypotheses

The intention is that these questions are used as triggers to help practitioners reflect on whether they have explored all possible hypotheses during an assessment and have explained this thoroughly in their assessment report.

Hypothesising at the early stage of involvement

- ■ Can you develop some hypotheses – at least four? (More if you can – keep them broad, not just single-incident based ones.)

- ■ What knowledge and information are the hypotheses based on (for example, theory, research, observation, assumptions, information given, hearsay)?

- ■ What actions will you take to test out your hypotheses?

- ■ Can you construct an action plan for testing them, with timescales identifying the methods you will use?

- ■ Who will be involved in gathering information to test out your hypotheses?

- ■ How will you seek evidence to disprove (disconfirm) your hypotheses?

- ■ What will you use to help you decide how to weight the value of different hypotheses?

Reviewing hypotheses mid-way through an assessment

- ■ Have you been able to test out all of the original hypotheses?

- ■ Are you satisfied that you have tested the hypotheses rigorously and you haven't simply sought out information to confirm your original hypotheses?

- ■ Of the original hypotheses, which have you discarded and why?

- ■ Have any new hypotheses emerged?

- ■ What methods are you going to use to test out the new hypotheses?

Evaluating hypotheses towards the end of the assessment

- ■ Are you satisfied that you have tested all the available hypotheses sufficiently rigorously?

- ■ Are you able to demonstrate, in your assessment report, the methods you have used to test out the hypotheses and why you have discarded or retained each one?

- ■ Are there some hypotheses that you have not been able to test out because of the unavailability of sufficient information or lack of time or access to key people?

- ■ If so, are further enquiries indicated beyond the point of this assessment?

- ■ If so, what form do you recommend these should take?

Hypothesising

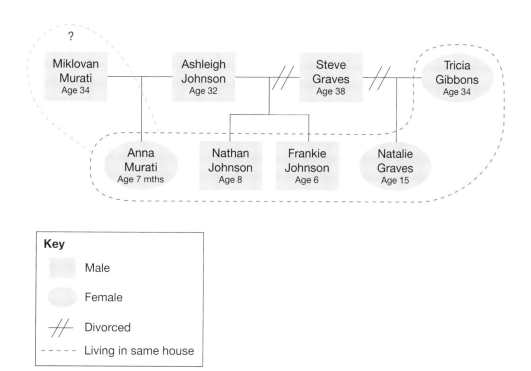

Name	Age	Gender	Ethnicity	Status/relationship
Tricia Gibbons	34	female	White British	mother
Miklovan Murati	34	male	Albanian	Anna's father
Anna Murati	7 months	female	dual-heritage Albanian/English	daughter of Tricia & Miklovan
Frankie Johnson	6	male	dual-heritage (African-Caribbean/White British)	son of Tricia & Ashleigh
Nathan Johnson	8	male	dual-heritage (same as Frankie)	son of Tricia & Ashleigh
Natalie Graves	15	female	White British	daughter of Tricia & Steve Graves
Ashleigh Johnson	32	male	African-Caribbean	Nathan and Frankie's father
Steve Graves	38	male	White British	Natalie's father

Tricia is a 34-year-old woman who lives with her partner and her four children in Sandley, a metropolitan borough in the West Midlands. The family moved into the borough from a neighbouring one about eight months ago, just before the birth of Anna.

Miklovan is the father of the youngest child, Anna. He is Albanian and, as far as the professionals are aware, Miklovan was previously an asylum seeker. However, further details around his current immigration status are unknown to the professionals. He has lived with Tricia for the last two years.

The father of Frankie and Nathan is Tricia's ex-husband, Ashleigh, who now lives in Birmingham. He has some contact with the boys. This usually occurs when he rings and arranges to pick up the boys to take them over to Birmingham for the weekend or during the school holidays. The arrangement is a loose one with no particular pattern to it.

Natalie's father, Tricia's first husband Steve, is serving a twelve-year prison sentence for armed robbery. He has not lived with Tricia since Natalie was two years old, although he was having regular monthly contact with Natalie until he went to prison last year.

The referral

The referral has been made by the health visitor because of concerns about Anna's development. She is underweight and has dropped below the 25th centile (she was at the 50th centile at her previous check). She was growing well for the first three months, but her progress has slowed in the last four. A referral has been made to the child development clinic for developmental tests to try to establish if there is any organic cause for the developmental slow down.

Tricia maintains that Anna is feeding well, but the health visitor is concerned because the house is in a filthy state after having been reasonably tidy and clean initially when she started visiting. Anna is often wearing a heavily soiled nappy when the health visitor visits. Tricia has become withdrawn and uncommunicative, possibly depressed. The health visitor has observed a lack of affection and engagement with Anna, although she has observed Natalie picking her up and playing with her when she has been there. Tricia does not seem to be particularly responsive to the health visitor's concerns about Anna's development.

The health visitor is not sure if Miklovan is still living with the family and says Tricia is evasive when asked. The health visitor hasn't seen him there for some time.

Checks with school reveal that they had been on the verge of making a referral to social services because of a build-up of recent concerns connected with the boys. Frankie is well behind the expected attainment levels for his age; he finds it difficult to cope in the classroom setting and seems very angry, often fighting with other children. Nathan is more settled and doing okay, but both boys often turn up late and are collected late. They have a lot of time off and they are often grubby and unkempt. Frankie recently commented to a classroom assistant that his mum was upset because Miklovan had 'gone off on one again' and had 'smashed Nathan's PlayStation and gone to Bolton'.

Natalie is in Year 11 at secondary school, her GCSE year, but has had a lot of absences recently, which have caused concern in relation to her forthcoming exams, and coursework completion deadlines. Otherwise, the school sees her as a quiet, unassuming girl. Parents have not attended open evenings and phone calls home have had little response.

Examples of the different hypotheses generated and plans for testing them out*

Table 2.2

Hypotheses	Methods for testing hypotheses
Domestic violence	Ask Tricia, Physical evidence, Talk to children, Speak to domestic violence team, Speak to other agencies, Investigate previous relationships, Talk to extended family, Use Fahlberg scale
Miklovan has a positive influence on the family. Things have deteriorated recently since he left	Ask Tricia, Talk to children, Make visits at different times of day, Make unannounced visits, Talk to schools, Clarify with health visitor
Tricia is depressed (post-natal depression?)	Use HV Edinburgh questionnaire, Check post-natal depression score, Use Adult Wellbeing Scale (DH and others 2000), Ask Tricia how she feels, Use observation, Liaise with other agencies, Talk to children, Talk to health visitor
Financial difficulties/impact of poverty	Talk to Tricia, Look at financial information/examine benefits take-up, etc.
On the run from CP registration in another authority; or Miklovan's unknown whereabouts linked to uncertain immigration status	Checks with other agencies and other authorities
Organic cause of failure to thrive	Check HV records, Refer to child development clinic
Socially excluded family, therefore more vulnerable	Talk to Tricia, Talk to children, Explore networks of support, such as neighbours' groups
Physical abuse of children esp. Frankie and Nathan by Miklovan	Look for physical evidence, Examine agency checks for previous incidents, Talk to Frankie and Nathan
Natalie is a young carer	Talk to Natalie on her own, Talk to Natalie with Tricia, Explain 'young carer' definitions and introduce local services

* These hypotheses and plans to carry them out were developed by groups participating in a practice development exercise, based on Case study 2.2, during the Putting analysis into assessment project.

As with the previous activity, the above are simply examples of answers generated during the practice development exercise with participants on the Putting analysis into assessment project. They are not right or wrong. The intention is to maintain a needs-based approach to making enquires and, by keeping the possible hypotheses in mind when planning enquiries, there is perhaps more likelihood of asking questions and talking to people who may provide greater insight into the circumstances of the different family members through a variety of routes.

Practice development session 3

Hypothesising

Aim

To help practitioners understand the meaning of hypothesising during assessment and to test this out in practice.

Method

a)   Begin **either** by asking participants what they understand by the word *hypothesis.*

b)   **Or** invite participants to form pairs to discuss hypothesising. Tell them to prepare answers, to be shared with the full group, to questions such as: What is hypothesising? When should it happen? Who should be involved?

c)   Whether the task was performed by the participants in pairs or otherwise, invite participants to share their answers. Record the answers, without questioning them, on a flip chart.

d)   Explain to the participants what hypothesising is (using notes on hypothesising from this section; or the relevant slides from Presentation 2, see Appendix, or download from www.ncb.org.uk/resources/support).

e)   Distribute Case study 2.3 on Hypothesising or a case study of your own choosing, or, if a team is participating in the course, one drawn from one of the team's real cases.

f)   Organise the participants into groups of four and distribute the Questions to assist in hypothesising (page 28). Ask the groups to work through the bullet points in the section called Hypothesising at the early stage of involvement. Record their points on a flip chart.

g)   Reconvene the full group. Invite each small group to take one hypothesis and to run through how they would test it out. Encourage discussion on how to incorporate this approach into the timescales of initial and core assessments. Ask whether they foresee any difficulties and how they might overcome them. Record all the positive actions suggested for overcoming the potential difficulties.

3. Conducting the assessment

Needs analysis

This section deals with the importance of taking a needs-led approach to assessment. Furthermore, it looks at how taking a holistic approach to the needs of children from the outset of assessment, assists with analysis throughout the process.

Practitioners are, on the whole, conversant with the needs-led approach to assessment – the basic principle of assessment. This section, however, offers an opportunity to focus on needs with practitioners to provide them with both a timely reminder and an opportunity to step back and consider how needs-led their own practice and the culture of their team and agency actually are.

As mentioned in the Introduction, *The Framework for the Assessment of Children in Need and Their Families* (Department of Health and others 2000) was intended to provide a systematic way of analysing, understanding and recording what is happening to children and young people – both within their families and in the wider context of the community in which they live – in order to be able to make professional judgements about them. These judgements include whether the child is in need or suffering significant harm; what actions must be taken; and what services would best meet the needs of that particular child and family.

Part III of The Children Act 1989 lays out the duty on local authorities to provide services to safeguard and promote the welfare of children in need and provides a definition of a child in need, deeming that a child is in need if:

a) he is unlikely to achieve or maintain or to have the opportunity of achieving or maintaining a reasonable standard of health or development without the provision for him of services by a local authority *or*

b) his health and development is likely to be significantly impaired or further impaired without the provision for him of such services *or*

c) he is disabled.

The Children Act 1989 set out a framework within which children in need and their families would be provided with services in order to ensure the child achieved his or her expected developmental outcomes. Research studies, commissioned by the Department of Health on the working of the child protection system in England and Wales and published in *Child Protection: Messages from research* in 1995, showed that child protection concerns continued to be the main trigger by which families gained access to services.

In many authorities it was only if there was evidence of potential significant harm that access to family support services could be gained, which was directly against the intentions of Part III of the Act. The absence of a consistent approach to the assessment of children in need meant that similar children were being treated very differently in different authorities.

The Assessment Framework was introduced as part of the government's broad aim of improving outcomes for children in need and, in particular, to support the objective for children's social services in 1999: *to ensure that referral and assessment processes discriminate effectively between different types and levels of need and produce a timely service response* (DH and others 2000).

The Assessment Framework takes the broad approach to identifying children in need that the Children Act 1989 intended. It is a conceptual map to gather and analyse information about children and families, in order to determine if a child is in need and what services are required to address those needs. It is informed by extensive research and practice knowledge and is based on the following principles, that is, that assessments should be:

- child-centred

- rooted in child development

- designed to ensure equality of opportunity

- ecological in their approach

- carry an assumption of close inter-agency working

- viewed as a continuing process

- carried out in parallel with other actions, including the provision of services.

Needs versus risks?

Some have argued that the emphasis on children's needs in the Assessment Framework dangerously ignores risk to children, and specifically the risk of significant harm (Calder and others 2004). However, focusing only on risks has severe limitations.

There had been something of a preoccupation, over the twenty years or so prior to the development of the Assessment Framework, with models for risk assessment that tended to stress family dysfunction rather than strengths (Seden and others 2001). This is in some part explained by the public and professional anxiety response resulting from highly publicised child-death inquiries; and a desire to be able to predict the risks to children's welfare associated with 'parental dangerousness'. Risk assessment schedules offer a range of predictors and factors derived from what, in the past, have contributed to dangerous actions. They provide a map of clusters of factors which, when aggregated, indicate cause for concern (Seden and others 2001).

A number of commentators have, however, drawn attention to the problems thrown up by over-reliance on such materials. There are reasons to be cautious about their use. Literature from the United States has identified problems of inadequate implementation, evaluation, and difficulties of working with complex and variable data.

It is actually impossible to decide with 100 per cent accuracy whether, and to what degree, a particular constellation of factors within the family or within individual caregivers will constitute risk of harm to a child. Over-reliance on risk assessment instruments has been shown to be problematic (Munro 2002). Risk assessment instruments developed within one population may have little relevance when transported to another and it is dangerous to apply tools and schedules without due regard to the individual characteristics of the child and family concerned. Wald and Woolverton (1990, p.505 in Cash 2001) said: *In the hands of unskilled workers these instruments may actually produce worse decisions.*

Reporting on a systematic review of studies of outcomes following identification of abuse or neglect, in order to assess the likelihood of a repeat of abuse or other poor outcomes, Jones and others (2006) highlight some of the possible factors that may increase risks of abuse to a child. However they state ultimately that, although these factors might be applied to practice, they cannot be done so *in a precise or numerical way*. They go on to highlight the limitations of numerical and actuarial approaches and offer the following comment.

> It is highly unlikely that the actuarial approach will take us further than the realm of guidance for a practitioner's individual decision-making simply because of the complex and multi-factorial nature of individual cases in the real world.

Instead, the authors urge openness as an approach so as to allow for reflection and external scrutiny.

Munro (2002) also suggests the following.

> The overwhelming message from the discussion of accurate risk assessment is that child protection workers should be very cautious in their claims to be able to predict abuse. This has implications for any message conveyed to the public about their skills.

Munro goes on to argue for a standards-based approach, which emphasises transparency of decision-making.

> Not that they [decisions] are infallible but that they can be shown to be reasonable estimates based on the evidence that was available at the time.

In short, there is a place for checklists and schedules as helpful mapping tools but they cannot be used without professional judgement. Cash (2001), in an analysis of research about risk-assessment instruments, says that risk-assessment instruments are not a panacea for decision-making in child welfare. He states that decisions should optimally be made through a combination of both empirical evidence [science] and practice wisdom [art], as one without the other is incomplete. He also suggests that the synergy of art and science allows for a more holistic and effective assessment.

This toolkit stresses that a holistic assessment of needs, using all three domains of the framework, allows for a comprehensive and holistic exploration of those factors that potentially promote or compromise the welfare and safety of the child or children being assessed; and takes into account contextual effects within the family and community systems.

A needs-led approach

A realistic approach to balancing needs and risks of harm is one that adheres to the principles outlined above and combines this with a thorough analysis of the information gathered.

Research by Sinclair (2001, in Seden and others 2001) on the language of need, attempted to identify the language actually used by practitioners to describe the needs of children they were working with to see if patterns and groupings emerged.

This work, commissioned by the Department of Health to inform the development of the Assessment Framework, found that social workers on the whole had little difficulty in applying a needs-focused analysis to their cases. They tended to use language (see examples in italics) which focused on the following aspects (shown in bold text).

■ **The causes:** *the break up of the family and the rejection by both parents; having been sexually abused, she's extra vulnerable.*

■ **Manifestation:** *she was self-harming, she was liable to cause herself some sort of permanent damage.* Or

■ **Symptomology:** *he has all these needs about his behaviours but all of these were based on his emotional difficulties, his sense of self.*

And they were described in one of the following ways (shown in bold).

- **Developmental terms:** *developmentally there were issues of neglect ... of weight loss.* OR

- **Context or circumstances** within which the child was living: *he lives with a single-parent mother who finds it difficult to cope with aspects of his behaviour.*

The research highlighted the multiplicity, complexity and compounding nature of the needs of the children referred to; and the fact that multiplicity of needs may be as important as severity of need. This research again highlights the importance of taking a holistic approach – an approach that is not limited to looking at only one aspect of a child's life experience.

Several years after the implementation of the Assessment Framework, research by Cleaver and Walker (2004) on its implementation suggests that there are ongoing concerns about the ability of practitioners to analyse needs during the assessment process. It also suggests that, whilst most managers identified an improvement in assessments within their agencies as a result of the framework, *a considerable proportion of social workers expressed anxiety about their ability to carry out assessments, particularly how to analyse the information they collected during the assessment and collaborative working with colleagues from other agencies.*

The assessment triangle is now widely understood as the model which identifies the holistic needs of a child in the three different domains: developmental needs; parent's capacity to meet those needs; and the family and environmental context in which the child is living. But time pressures, agency policy and pressures from referrers all contribute to a tendency to slot children and families into existing services, rather than to take the time to make a proper analysis of the needs of a child or children in a family and to decide what interventions or services are most likely to meet those needs.

Despite initial concerns, the analysis of need activity, which was carried out with practitioners early on in the project, was welcomed by the practitioners. They saw it as an opportunity to reflect together as a team on the degree to which the concept of need remained at the heart of the assessment process. The activity is described in detail in the Needs analysis practice development session (page 42).

The Needs and outcomes form (page 37) was designed as part of the National Children's Bureau's Care planning project (Williams and McCann 2006). The three forms designed are available on the *Care Planning for Looked After Children* CD-Rom, and are designed for identifying needs and planned outcomes; developing care plans to meet those needs; and producing an action plan. The Needs and outcomes form is included in here.

When practitioners and managers were introduced to the form in the course of the Putting analysis into assessment project, they thought it would be useful as an informal tool for planning, reflection and supervision.

The two case studies (page 39), Sammy and Danny, were used with practitioners, to test their ability to identify needs as opposed to services or inputs. In the practice development exercise, they were asked to identify Sammy's and Danny's needs in relation to the developmental dimensions.

PRACTICE TOOL: NEEDS AND OUTCOMES FORM

	Needs Please summarise your professional judgement about the child's needs	Outcomes Decide which aspects of the child's needs should be addressed and describe the outcomes to be achieved. Set a realistic timescale for each outcome.
Health		
Education/ cognitive and language development		
Emotional and behavioural development		
Identity		
Family and social relationships		

Putting Analysis into Assessment

	Needs Please summarise your professional judgement about the child's needs	Outcomes Decide which aspects of the child's needs should be addressed and describe the outcomes to be achieved. Set a realistic timescale for each outcome.
Social presentation		
Self-care skills		
Parenting capacity		
Family and environmental factors		

Putting Analysis into Assessment

CASE STUDY 3.1

Danny

Danny is three. His mother misuses alcohol but her care of her children seemed just about adequate until she met a new partner. He also drank heavily and was violent. There was a drunken fight between Danny's mother and her partner in a local pub and Danny's mother sustained a head injury and was taken to hospital.

Police were involved and found Danny and his seven-year-old sister, Marie, at home on their own. They were grubby and miserable and the police took them into police protection. They have been placed with a local foster carer who says that Marie is worried about her mum and keeps trying to take charge of Danny. Danny is reported to be small for his age and his speech is delayed. He seems to look to Marie for care and affection. He is not toilet-trained and keeps asking where his mummy is.

Danny's needs are ...

CASE STUDY 3.2

Sammy

Sammy is five and the only child of a mother with schizophrenia. She is devoted to Sammy and cares for him well as long as she takes her medication. Sammy has just started school and the school says that, despite appearing chatty and polite, they feel he is an anxious child. He finds it hard to play with other children and is clingy with the teachers. He says he sleeps in his mum's bed because of the ghosts in the house. She has started turning up during the school day to check he is okay.

Sammy's needs are ...

In the following table, the right-hand column shows some of the responses given. We found that whilst the project participants were relatively needs-focused, there were usually numerous examples given of services or interventions as opposed to needs. The responses in italics are the ones that were more service- or input-focused.

| Case study 3.1: Danny | Danny is three. His mother misuses alcohol but her care of her children seemed just about adequate until she met a new partner. He also drank heavily and was violent. There was a drunken fight between Danny's mother and her partner in a local pub and Danny's mother sustained a head injury and was taken to hospital. Police were involved and found Danny and his seven-year-old sister, Marie, at home on their own. They were grubby and miserable and the police took them into police protection. They have been placed with a local foster carer who says that Marie is worried about her mum and keeps trying to take charge of Danny. Danny is reported to be small for his age and his speech is delayed. He seems to look to Marie for care and affection. He is not toilet-trained and keeps asking where his mummy is. Danny's needs are ... | **Health**
Good physical care
Health check/assessment
Good paediatric assessment
Assessment of health needs
LAC Health assessment
Developmental check
Health visitor
High standard of physical and emotional care *[foster carers]*

Education
Needs stimulation
Stimulation and socialisation
Needs help understanding the situation
Assessment of his mother's ability to change and provide safe care
Speech therapy

Emotional and behavioural development
Emotional warmth and attachment
Consistent stimulating environment to help develop age-appropriate skills
Help to feel safe
Developmental assessment

Identity
Exploration of extended family

Family and social relationships
Needs a sense of family ... belonging to someone somewhere
Appropriate relationship with sister Marie
Contact with mother and other significant family members
Consistent parenting
Work with mother and stepfather on parenting skills
Make links with extended family and establish if they can care for him – kinship assessment
Explicit contract with carer re day to day work with the child

Social presentation
Speech therapy

Self-care skills
Toilet training |

| Case study 3.2: Sammy | Sammy is five and the only child of a mother with schizophrenia. She is devoted to Sammy and cares for him well as long as she takes her medication. Sammy has just started school and the school says that, despite appearing chatty and polite, they feel he is an anxious child. He finds it hard to play with other children and is clingy with the teachers. He says he sleeps in his mum's bed because of the ghosts in the house. She has started turning up during the school day to check he is okay. Sammy's needs are … | **Health**
Maintaining health
To maintain existing good health
Diet, exercise
Access to health services
Routine health surveillance
Individual work to identify need
Mum needs a mental health assessment!
Assessment of Sammy's mental health/attachment in order to provide appropriate services and the impact of his mum's mental health

Education
Stability and security in education placement to reduce anxiety
To learn and be exposed to age-appropriate learning opportunities and experiences
Needs to feel secure in school
Social opportunities
To attend school
Classroom assistant
Establish what school actually means to Sammy
Educational Psychologist assessment

Emotional and behavioural development
Self-esteem
Relationship-building
Play and self-occupancy skills
Stability
Security
Boundaries. Appropriate separation from his mum
Age-appropriate socialising – free from responsibility to and for mother
Friendships
Needs security and to feel safe
Assessment of attachment issues
Referral to young carers' project

Identity
Has he got one of his own?
Needs help to establish one
A sense of growing independence from mother
Freedom to pursue personal identity separate from his mother
Mother to be secure and mentally well in order to focus on him
Assess if any issues

Family and social relationships
Exposure to relatives and friends
Opportunities for wider experience in safe environment
Support to come to terms with mother's illness
Needs security and probably wider network, e.g. community/family
Assessment of what family networks there are?

Social presentation
Psychological assessment
Referral to after-school club

Self-care skills
Needs to fit into peer group
To be relaxed, secure in self |

Practice development session 4

Needs analysis

Aim

To introduce a model for needs-led analysis and planning for children and their families; and to provide an opportunity to test this out in practice.

Method

Introduction

- Introduce the theme of the session by showing Presentation 3 (see Appendix or download from www.ncb.org.uk/resources/support). Preferably expand on it in the following ways.

  - Mention that inspection reports have commented that it is not always clear how services provided meet needs.

  - Make the point that consideration of needs is very relevant to the assessment of family and friends (explain, if necessary, that it is important when assessing a child's needs to look at whether the family can meet them and what kind of support they would require to do so).

  - Explain that, if the child's needs are stated explicitly, it helps children and their parents to understand what must be done to meet needs, and what the purpose of the intervention is.

  - In analysing the situation it is helpful to remain focused on the child's needs rather than being drawn too much into the parents' difficulties.

Stage 1 of the decision-making

- Invite the participants to form pairs or groups of three.

- Distribute the Case studies 3.1 (Danny) and 3.2 (Sammy) so that each group has either Danny or Sammy. Give out the Needs–Outcomes form (page 37) to each participant.

- Ask the participants to look at the case study they have been given and, in their pairs or groups, to identify all the child's needs under each of the developmental dimensions of the assessment triangle (those indicated on the Needs–outcomes form). Make it clear that they should record **each need** on a separate sticky note.

- Tell them they have 10 minutes to complete this.

- Meanwhile, prepare two flip charts, one for Danny, one for Sammy. (Or, if you have prepared your own case studies, record their names instead.) Write the seven dimension titles on each flip chart, leaving space under each dimension title for participants to attach sticky notes.

- After 10 minutes, ask participants to come to the flip chart and place sticky notes under the child's name and specific dimensions.

- Offer feedback on the activity. Invite participants to disagree if they wish, and reassure them that picking up on issues is not meant as personal criticism.

■ Comment positively on where clear needs have been identified (such as the need to increase self-esteem, feeling safe, access to peer relationships) and also note where services have been identified (such as paediatric assessment, counselling, family centre).

■ Give information on the theory that underpins this activity, referring to the notes above if necessary.

Stage 2 of the decision-making

■ Give the participants an example of what an outcome (in relation to a need) might be, for example:

   – **Need** – child to have social relationships with peers.

   – **Outcome** – Child has two friends at school with whom she/he regularly plays with at break times OR child attends playgroup twice a week and successfully mixes socially with children his/her age.

■ Remind participants that they are not to identify services to meet needs – yet.

■ Invite participants to form pairs (preferably where they both know or could be working with the same child) and think of a case they are involved with.

■ Check that each couple is focusing on the case of one child and are not concerning themselves with siblings. Ask them to identify the child's needs first, then add outcomes using the Needs–outcomes form. Ask them to think what the child/parent/carer/ teacher/other professionals would identify as the child's needs and good outcomes, and add them.

■ Conclude this part by mentioning resilience as a key aspect of the desired outcomes. Explain that the planned outcome should not just be to minimise the damage to children but to positively promote their well-being. So practitioners would need to think about and include preparation for any separations; and ways of promoting trusting relationships, friendships and success at school, hobbies and interests.

Stage 3 of the decision-making

■ Invite participants to identify the services that may be able to meet the various needs that have been identified and achieve the desired outcomes. Point out that some services might meet more than one need.

■ There may be needs identified for which there are no existing services. If this is the case, ask the participants to describe the type of service they believe might meet these needs. Ask them to draw on knowledge and experience of other areas or from evidence-based research.

■ If you wish, record the services on the flip chart.

Feedback

■ Ask participants how they felt the activity went.

■ Ask: Was it hard to focus on the child's needs?

■ Invite each group to give one example of a child's need, a planned outcome and a service to meet it.

- Ask: Do you feel that slowing down the decision-making stages added anything to their usual mode of operation?

- Ask: Did it mean that they might select different types of services or different constellations of service to meet children's needs?

- Invite participants to consider how the clear focus on needs might assist with analysis throughout the assessment – for example, in terms of agreeing the approach with the family or explaining a particular course of action in a report.

- Ask: How might this approach be helpful to you in day-to-day practice? And in supervision, arguing for resources, etc.

- Point out that there are additional planning forms on *the Care Planning for Looked After Children* CD-Rom (Williams and McCann 2006) – tools that allow for service planning and action planning.

Signs of safety

This section looks at the need to do more to ensure that assessments are not too skewed by an over-concentration on risk of harm; and that families strengths are sufficiently acknowledged and harnessed throughout the course of assessment and intervention. It goes on to include a brief introduction to the Signs of safety approach put forward by Turnell and Edwards (1999).

The last few sections have looked at the ease with which social workers can unwittingly jump to decisions that are unduly influenced by the context in which they are operating, such as service constraints and fear of making mistakes. This tendency extends to the whole approach that social workers take to their assessments and to their relationships with all family members being assessed.

Whilst a desire to work in partnership with families and service users is hardly a new idea, it is still, in reality, hard to translate meaningfully into practice.

In recent years it has been widely acknowledged and demonstrated, for example in *Child Protection: Messages from research* (DH 1995), that in England the emphasis in child care social work has been more on child protection than on preventative family support approaches. Whilst the *Framework for Assessment of Children in Need and their Families* (Department of Health and others 2000) is intended to enshrine a needs-based approach, where strengths are considered in tandem with risk of harm, pressure on services means that often the bulk of allocated cases are those where some risk of harm or severe needs are present. With this, the tendency has perhaps been to over-emphasise investigative and forensic procedures.

Parton (1996, in Turnell and Edwards 1999) argues that this:

> effectively becomes a blaming system, the primary purpose being to establish who is accountable for any given incident.

It is hardly surprising that true partnership-working with parents and family members is such a difficult area when the stakes in children and families' social work are so high. One of the greatest conundrums of child protection, the authors of the Signs of safety approach argue, is:

> How to recognise the occasional families that cannot be assisted or coerced to provide increased safety, without demonising excessive numbers of other families with the same, though inappropriate label.

When social workers are concerned about a child's welfare, an inadequate understanding of the parent whom they consider to be responsible for that child, can often lead to skewed and over-simplistic conclusions. If a child's experience is in the range of the 'thresholds' of likely or actual significant harm, social workers don't want to mess about. They need to do something about it. To get answers and clarity, so as to *act* as is their duty. Legal and policy constraints form almost invisible walls around their focus and thinking. This is for a good reason. If they did not have the clarity of message – that is, *if a child is or is likely to be suffering significant harm it is our legal duty to protect them* – then their good intentions of fairness, and natural resistance to coping with uncertainty, could lead to them becoming paralysed by that uncertainty or 'woolly' in thinking, and therefore to becoming variable in their priorities and responses. While the social workers sit and wonder, more children might get harmed; or those being harmed may not get help from social workers to prevent, minimise or stop them from coming to harm.

Partnership therefore, whilst its worthiness is indisputable, can easily be in danger of being only surface deep. The social worker might, for example, show a parent the report they write and give the parent sufficient time to comment, suggest alternatives and have their views recorded before signing it. The social worker might give the parent information about their rights, try to involve them in formulating and carrying out protection plans or facilitate a Family Group Conference, none of which are to be minimised. However, just as often social workers might gradually 'accept' that they 'cannot' involve a semi-absent, alleged substance-misusing father. They give up on him and, after deciding that the mother (who tells a health visitor one thing and the social worker another) is not being honest or 'able to work in partnership', they start making statements (literally or figuratively) about her denying her problem, lacking insight, and being 'unable to put her child's needs first'. Such statements are weighty and have powerful implications, but are in danger of being used perhaps too readily or with insufficient qualification.

Turnell and Edwards (1999) highlighted feedback, gained from parents in consumer studies, in which parents described the feeling of being seen as a 'case', especially in evidence gathering interviews. The emphasis on identifying deficits and weaknesses – rather than strengths and resources – contributes to families' defensiveness; and a steady stream of professionals focusing on what is wrong can undermine a family's sense of its capacities and capabilities (Ban 1992, in Turnell and Edwards 1999). They felt that if they were identified as bad parents early on, it was very difficult if not impossible to get workers to see them differently or as 'capable' later on.

These issues are not easily solved and good intentions alone are not enough on their own to mitigate against the many and real pressures on social workers, which may lead to giving up on partnership too easily. The following approach is just one example of a model social workers can draw from to help in the conscious pursuit of balance and partnership within their work.

The practice principles and review form

Signs of Safety: A solution and safety orientated approach to child protection (Turnell and Edwards 1999) has 'promoting partnership' as its underpinning principle. The approach emphasises the need to try and establish 'collaboration', with service users as opposed to a 'helping relationship'. The approach involves: *turning away from deficits and focusing on the discovery of resources, however small, to expose building blocks for change.*

The approach was born out of the Teen Link project in Perth in the early 1990s. There were only three workers who had a remit to see hundreds of families in a year. In order to meet these demands, they adopted a Brief Therapy approach. Social workers, who became aware of the project's success with clients, developed – in partnership with them – a model designed to bring brief therapy principles and methods into child protection work. Their approach offers a structure to facilitate the integration of family *and* professional knowledge, from intake through to closure. They see partnership and paternalism as being on a continuum.

> Partnership exists when both the statutory agency and the family cooperate and make efforts to achieve specific, mutually understood goals. Partnership cannot be categorised by an equitable distribution of power between family and agency. One demonstration of this is the fact that the agency will almost always begin the relationship and necessarily defines when it will conclude.

> Turnell & Edwards 1999

It is not possible or appropriate to outline the approach here in all its detail or to describe 'how to do it'. In the case of the collaboration in Perth, a full programme of training took place with the social workers involved. But within the approach are a series of practice principles and a form to aid assessment, which can be useful to those social workers concerned with issues of partnership and ensuring they assess safety as well as danger.

The following is a précis of the Practice principles that form a backdrop to the assessments, as described by Turnell and Edwards (1999).

Practice principles that build partnerships

1. Respect service recipients as people worth doing business with (not *to*)
    This is not to be confused with naïve practice, a fear of challenging or a rule of optimism.

2. Cooperate with the person not the abuse
    This involves acknowledging strengths as well as weaknesses and not treating individuals as 'another job lot'. This includes showing awareness and sensitivity about the stress brought on by the assessment process or investigation itself.

3. Recognise that cooperation is possible even where coercion is required
    The authors stress the importance of recognising inequality of power but using it sensitively in a 'considered and skilful fashion'.

4. Recognise that all families have signs of safety
    Families are often 'pigeon-holed' and seen primarily in the context of their 'problem' label and this is not weighed up with other aspects of their behaviour and being.

5. Maintain a focus on safety
    The Signs of Safety approach suggests focusing on goals and talking about 'presence' rather than 'absence', for example telling the mother of a neglected child that she needs to be in earshot and eyesight of the baby at all times.

6. Learn what the service recipient wants
    This refers to the importance of harnessing the motivations of service users. For example, the client might not agree with the social workers concerns but might be motivated by wanting the worker 'out of his or her hair' and be willing to make changes for that end which might fit with the workers' explicitly safety-focused goals.

7. Always search for detail
    The authors stress the importance of obtaining detailed and balanced information – that is, thorough, negative and positive, from sources inside and outside the family. This serves as an antidote to naïve practice and provides the best basis for realistic assessment and case plans. Also, thorough exploration will increase the chances of identifying antecedents, consequences, patterns, feelings and opportunities for change.

8. Focus on creating small change
    The tradition of Brief Therapy holds that change is continuous and therefore one (small) change will inevitably lead to further change. Frequently, trying to achieve big goals quickly leads to frustration. A focus on specific, small changes can be more useful, even if only for the reason that people have a sense of something being achieved.

9. Don't confuse case details with judgements
    This approach stresses the difference between an event and the value or meaning ascribed to it. For example, if a mother walks out of a meeting she could be labelled as uncooperative and future information might be used to 'prove' this further; when in fact she had had a terrible week, was being asked questions she'd answered many times before, and had a view (perhaps founded) that those present had already 'made up their minds'.

10. Offer choices
    Where possible, the likelihood of a family engaging constructively with a process is heightened by having choices to minimise (but not eradicate) the power differential. The worker needs to be clear about the non-negotiable aspects of the case however, for example, 'We need to discuss these issues with you today. Can you suggest the best time and place for us to meet during the day?'

11. **Treat the interview as a forum for change**

    The interview is the intervention – the authors argue that even child protection investigations can be therapeutic. The investigations can develop a family's understanding of issues and offer support and education. The case plan and interventions are the 'icing on the cake'. The interview is the relationship between worker and family and is the principal vehicle for change.

Finally, we are reminded to treat the practice principles as aspirations rather than assuming that, because the worker agrees with them in theory, they are being adhered to.

In addition to the Practice principles outlined above, Turnell and Edwards listed the following *Six practice elements*, which attempt to translate the principles into practice behaviours or values that should guide social workers' responses and actions in the assessment process.

The following is a précis of the practice elements described by Turnell and Edwards (1999).

1. **Understand the position of each family member**
    This includes their position in relation to the problem, the solution, and the statutory agency. For example: regarding the problem (*I was hit as a child and it never did me any harm*); the solution (*I don't need to talk, I just need some practical help*); and the statutory agency (*If I tell them the truth they'll take my child away*). A person's position includes their strongly held values, beliefs and the meanings they attach to things. Once the social worker *thinks* they have established the position of the person, they should always repeat it back to them to check this out.

    The authors liken understanding the position to understanding the plot in a play. Once you 'get' the characters, the plot and their actions make more sense.

2. **Exceptions to the neglect**
    'Exception questions' can be useful in eliciting information. For example: 'Tell me about the times when you get your child to listen to you without shouting at her.' This question is based on two assumptions: that the problem is not happening all the time; and that the person probably deals appropriately with the problem some of the time. Questioning such as this can uncover the absence of neglectful behaviour as well as the presence of safe and constructive behaviours. It is important to explore the details, asking the *how, when, where* and *what* of the incident; and to find out how confident the person is in their ability to repeat the exception.

    Exception questions can be useful at referral stage and beyond. For example: 'Can you tell me about times when (the parent) has responded appropriately in keeping the child safe? What did she do?' A positive answer will perhaps provide a way forward when meeting with the parent, and a negative one may alert the social worker to a potentially malicious referrer.

    In training, the authors suggest asking the question three times before deciding there is no answer – start by recognising that you [the social worker] are changing emphasis/shifting conversation, and only move on to exception questions after you have fully acknowledged what is being said about the problem or incident.

3. **Family strengths and resources**
    Michael White (1988) in Turnell and Edwards (1999) said that 'problem saturated description(s)' lead to impotence and hopelessness, which frequently happens to all concerned in child protection. By seeking to expand on this picture we can acknowledge some foundations on which to build the families strengths. Once again the answers to questions regarding strengths and resources can generate positive and constructive information and/or someone's inability to see anything positively can be highlighted.

Example question

We have been talking about some very serious matters. To give me a more balanced picture, can you tell me some of the things that you feel are good about this family?

4. **Focus on goals**
    Weick (1989, in Turnell and Edwards 1999) said: *The question is not what kind of life one has had but what kind of life one wants and then bringing to bear all the personal and social resources available to accomplish this goal.*

    Careful and explicit emphasis on the goals of both family and agency are the foundation of this approach, but the authors argue it is perhaps one of the most difficult to achieve and requires detailed knowledge of the case and careful thinking.

Examples of questions to elicit a family's safety goals

For our involvement with your family to be useful to you, what would need to happen? What would change in your family? What would change about your partner/your child?

The authors argue that, whilst the level of overlap between the goals of family member and those of professionals can vary greatly – and at times be hard to find – it is often possible to explore safety without complete agreement about the abuse or neglect. The goals should be firmed up ('concretised'), with specific, measurable steps identified towards achieving the necessary change.

5. **Scaling safety and progress**

By using scaling questions, workers can obtain information that is specific and detailed. This approach can be particularly useful with children.

Example of a scaling question

On a scale of 0–10, where 10 would mean things in this family are just the way you want them, and 0, that life could not be worse – where would you rate your family right now?

This approach is simple, direct, and easy to understand. Also, it calls for a very precise assessment of the situation from the service user – turning the paternalistic model of social worker as expert on its head. The approach often evokes very significant information.

This type of questioning has been criticised for putting too much onus on the family, or child, to assess their own situation; but it is only a tool, and information is not necessarily taken at face value. One woman, for example, rated her life a '4'; but when questioned about what positive things brought it up to a '4', she broke down and said it was really a '0' and began to admit and discuss in detail how depressed she had been feeling.

6. **Willingness, confidence and capacity**

For any plan to work with a family, consideration needs to be given to their engagement with it; their willingness, confidence and capacity to achieve it.

Examples of scaling questions to assess each of these areas

Willingness

Ask: *If I asked you to do_____, on a scale of 0–10, how willing would you be?*
Then: *What, if anything, would increase your willingness to do something about these problems?*

Capacity to take action

Ask: *On a scale of 0–10, how would you rate your ability to do something about these problems?*

Then: *What parts of these plans would you feel most able to try? What or who could help you do these things?*

Confidence

On a scale of 0–10, how confident are you that you (your family) can do things to make your child safer (stop the abuse)? What would increase your confidence?

There is a case example in the book about a concerned grandmother, who seemed to point all problems to her son-in-law (stepfather) until scaling questions revealed her concerns would only shift half a point if he were to be out of the family.

Finally, the Signs of safety approach provides a useful form – with a scale for safety and progress – on which to record the relative safety and danger as the social worker sees it during their assessment of a family. In practice, the form is designed to be used where the principles described have already influenced the work that has taken place. However, social workers who were unfamiliar with the principles prior to their participation on the Putting analysis into assessment project, were able in many cases to utilise the form straight away, applying it to assessments they were undertaking and their feedback was often positive.

Figure 3.1 A scaling form: Signs of safety assessment form

Signs of safety assessment and planning form

You may wish to spatially locate items between the danger and safety poles along this continuum.

Danger

List of all aspects that demonstrate likelihood of maltreatment (past, present or future)

Safety

List of all aspects that indicate safety (e.g. exceptions, strengths and resources, goals, willingness)

Safety and context scale

Safety scale: Given the danger and safety information, rate the situation on a scale of 0–10, where 0 means recurrence of similar or worse abuse/neglect is certain and 10 means that there is sufficient safety for the child for you to close the case.

Context scale: Rate this case on a scale of 0–10, where 10 means that this is not a situation where any action would be taken and 0 means this is the worst case of child abuse or neglect that the agency has seen.

Agency goals. What will the agency need to occur or be willing to close this case?

Family goals. What does the family want generally, and regarding safety?

Immediate progress. What would indicate to the agency that some small progress has been made?

Copyright © 1997 Steve Edwards and Andrew Turnell

Putting Analysis into Assessment

CASE STUDY 3.3

Signs of safety

Name	Age	Gender	Ethnicity	Relationship
Kayleigh Bell	11 months	female	Mixed Parentage	subject (White British/Black Caribbean)
Sophie Cousins	5 years	female	White British	half-sister
Darren Cousins	9 years	male	White British	half-brother
Danielle Cousins	25 years	female	White British	mother
Frank Cousins	41 years	male	White British	father of Darren & Sophie
Jared Bell	29 years	male	Black Caribbean	Kayleigh's father

Kayleigh Bell is referred to the duty social worker by the ward sister on the paediatric ward at the General Hospital. She was admitted earlier that day after Danielle took her to the GP because she was unwell with diarrhoea and sickness.

Kayleigh was found by the GP to be dehydrated and underweight for her age and stage of development. She appeared grubby, her nappy appeared not to have been changed for a long time and she had severe nappy rash. She was inappropriately dressed for the cold weather, listless and weak. She has been put on emergency rehydration/nutritional therapy and is undergoing further tests.

During the admission examination, the registrar discovered old bruising on her ribs and the tops of her legs for which there was no obvious explanation. The registrar thought from their appearance that they might be non-accidental in cause.

The registrar and ward sister tried talking to Danielle about Kayleigh's general health and about the bruising. The ward sister described Danielle as seeming very low, flat and unresponsive. However, Danielle did say that Kayleigh had never been a settled baby, had been sickly throughout her life and had developed diarrhoea recently as well. The registrar thought that Danielle appeared depressed and somewhat confused. Danielle did not reportedly know how the bruises might have been caused.

Darren and Sophie attended hospital with their mother. Sophie appeared to be fairly well nourished but grubby, unkempt and rather 'out of control'. Darren seemed to be trying to take charge of the situation: trying to control Sophie's behaviour by shouting at her; and holding his mother's arm – guiding her as though she was unwell. He tried to answer some of the questions that the registrar was asking. He said that his mum had been unwell and that he'd been making the baby's feed and feeding her for the last two weeks.

The family only moved to the area two weeks ago from a neighbouring borough where they had been known to Social Services. An Initial Assessment was carried out there about four months ago after Darren and Sophie's school had referred them due to Darren's poor school attendance, his tiredness, grubbiness, generally anxious demeanour and Sophie's disruptive behaviour in the school nursery. The assessment had identified that Danielle seemed depressed and that the family were in need of support. They had been referred to a local NCH project but they had moved out of the area just as a place became available.

The family was also known by the neighbouring authority from a few years prior to that, as there had been several reports to the police about domestic violence by Frank Cousins who had lived in the family at the time. The family had been visited at the time by Social Services but Frank Cousins had by this time moved out and no further action was taken.

Kayleigh's father, Jared, was apparently living with the family until six months ago when he returned to London, his home city. Danielle told the ward sister that she hadn't seen him for about four months.

Figure 3.2 An example of a completed Signs of safety form (in relation to Case Study 3.3)

Signs of safety assessment and planning form

You may wish to spatially locate items between the danger and safety poles along this continuum.

Danger

List of all aspects that demonstrate likelihood of maltreatment (past, present or future)
Sophie's behaviour
Current ill-health of child   Coping in-between referrals?
Underweight   Jared?
Grubby/unkempt
Nappy rash severe
Bruising
Unresponsiveness/low mood   Whilst providing some support to his mother Darren
No explanation for bruises   is taking responsibilities beyond his years & inadequate for baby.

Safety

List of all aspects that indicate safety (e.g. exceptions, strengths and resources, goals, willingness)
Cooperating with hospital   Danielle took child to GP
Danielle has shown willingness previously to accept help and background info from her previous borough – suggests she acknowledged that she was feeling depressed.
Danielle has registered with a GP within 2 weeks of moving

Safety and context scale

Safety scale: Given the danger and safety information, rate the situation on a scale of 0–10, where 0 means recurrence of similar or worse abuse/neglect is certain and 10 means that there is sufficient safety for the child for you to close the case.   5

Context scale: Rate this case on a scale of 0–10, where 10 means that this is not a situation where any action would be taken and 0 means this is the worst case of child abuse or neglect that the agency has seen.   4

Agency goals. What will the agency need to occur to be willing to close this case?
Kayleigh's physical care needs being met (able to be met) consistently and adequately.
Acknowledgement by Danielle of seriousness of concerns and concrete plans to address this.
Alleviation of concern re. bruising?

Family goals. What does the family want generally, and regarding safety?
Washing machine to help in dressing children appropriately.
Home to be organised – post move is in disarray.
Resume and continue contact with Jared.
Support in dealing with ex-partner who's recently become involved.

Immediate progress. What would indicate to the agency that some small progress has been made?
Danielle receiving support in her own right for depression – to visit GP about this.
Recovery of Kayleigh.
Home conditions resolved.
Agreement to referral to family centre for parenting support.
Acknowledgement of concerns for Darren and Sophie.

Copyright © 1997 Steve Edwards and Andrew Turnell

Putting Analysis into Assessment

Six practice elements

In working with this family, considerations could be given to applying the six practice elements. Examples of how the practice elements could relate to Case study 3.3 are given below.

1. *Understanding the position of each family member*
    Danielle tends to feel guilty and 'like a failure' when she becomes depressed and is struggling to cope. For this reason she has been reluctant to ask for help even though she has found life harder since she and Jared split up. She is not unwilling to accept help and would welcome it, but is slow to recognise that her depression affects her ability to judge what she needs.

    Darren views himself as the 'man of the house' and has been keen to look after his mother and siblings and reluctant to talk about his situation to anyone in case they 'interfere'. He has been struggling to look after Kayleigh and has always identified with his father and wondered if there is something wrong with him because his father was violent towards his mother.

2. *Exceptions to the neglect*
    It would be useful to explore with Danielle and the children how things have been previously. The previous involvement with the neighbouring borough would suggest that between Frank leaving the family home and the most recent referral, the family coped without social services hearing of any concerns from school or health visitors. This would indicate that Danielle might have been managing adequately during that time. One might ask Danielle, for example: 'Can you tell me about a time when you have felt happier and been proud of the way you have looked after the children?' Or Sophie could be asked about her achievements or when adults have praised her to counter the picture of her being 'out of control'.

3. *Family strengths and resources*
    Despite her depression and having only moved into the area two weeks ago, Danielle has managed to recognise the urgency of Kayleigh's condition and organised an emergency GP appointment. She has also shown a willingness, through the previous assessment, to accept support. Jared could possibly be a useful source of support to the family if arrangements were made; and Darren has shown a level of care and closeness in his behaviour towards his mother and sisters.

4. *Focus on goals*
    The difficulty that Danielle is having in meeting the basic care needs of her children have been compounded by the recent house move and her depression. There could well be some overlap between what she and the agency want; if, for example, Danielle wants the house to be organised, things unpacked and the washing machine plumbed in. She probably wants to feel better in herself, too, and to have more energy for the children. If Danielle was clear that she wanted Kayleigh home from hospital as soon as possible, this too would give common ground and a way forward for professionals to establish with her what would need to happen for this to take place.

5. *Scaling safety and progress*
    Scaling questions could provide a sense of Danielle's feelings over time. She could be asked to rate where she is now and then at previous times in her mood. She could also be asked what it would take for her to move up the scale a couple of notches.

    Similarly, Sophie and Darren could be asked about their views in this way, for example: 'If 10 is wonderful and 1 is terrible, how do you feel about living in your new house?' This could be built on, with questions arising from the response to ascertain what would make the difference, and how the situation now differs from the last house or when Jared lived in the home.

6. *Willingness, confidence and capacity*
    It would be very important to explore how committed, able and confident Danielle is to carry out any plans that emerge, as her low mood could lead to her agreeing passively to things but not in a meaningful way. Similarly, her lack of confidence and tendency to think she is a 'bad parent' could undermine her efforts. Specific questions about these areas, could include: 'On a scale of 1–10, how confident are you that you can keep this up (improvements in practical care of Kayleigh)?' and 'What would increase your confidence?'

    Some of these points may seem rather obvious and, of course, any considerations of safety factors and strengths would be weighed up alongside the fairly serious concerns that have arisen about Kayleigh, taking into account the established, or suspected, cause of her bruises. However, active pursuit of shared goals and strengths may increase the chances of a successful intervention.

Practice development session 5

The signs of safety approach

Aim

To introduce the Signs of safety approach; and to consider and test out how it might be usefully applied to practice and contribute to analysis and decision-making.

Methods

a)   Give a presentation to the participants on the Signs of safety approach, outlining its main messages and potential applications, using Presentation 4 (see Appendix or download from www.ncb.org.uk/resources/support).

b)   Distribute the Six practice elements (page 54), to the participants.

c)   Invite participants to form six groups or pairs.

d)   Give each group or pair a different practice element to focus on.

e)   Tell them to read the relevant part of the handout and plan a brief five-minute presentation, to be given to the wider group, in which they will convey what the practice element is and give examples of how it may be applied in their work.

f)   When the planning is complete, reconvene the full group, then invite each group or pair in turn to give their presentation.

g)   Distribute the Signs of safety assessment form (page 51).

h)   Run through the key elements of the form. Then invite participants to work, either individually or in small groups, on completing the form in relation to a real case they are involved with. If this is not possible, tell them to use Case study 3.3 instead (page 52). There are, of course, no right answers.

Involving children

How do children's contributions inform the analysis?

This section explores some of the issues that arise when practitioners are trying to incorporate and provide a balanced assessment of the views and perceptions of children within an analysis. It is widely accepted that enabling children's participation in matters that affect them is essential to good practice. However, this has never been easy to put into practice in a consistent and thorough manner. Following training courses relating to analysis and, in particular, discussions about where children's views fit into the analysis, practitioners and managers frequently say that often they do not have enough time to undertake sufficient direct work with children or to build up a trusting and consistent relationship. Sometimes they also highlight gaps in skills and resources too, but time it seems, in their view, is a significant factor.

Social workers are in a difficult position when it comes to engaging children meaningfully in their assessments. Some children and young people (although not so much young children) have negative views of social workers. This was highlighted by Butler and Williamson (1994), when they carried out a large-scale consultation with children and young people. Some of the criticisms children and young people made about social workers were that they were 'robotic', led by procedures and had fixed views and ways of doing things. They also often thought the social workers didn't listen properly, made false promises and 'spread things about'. This was also echoed in Morgan's (2005) study, where children and young people were reported to have said that if, for example, they were having problems at school, they were afraid that (as some had experienced) the social worker would 'immediately tell the school what you had said and that made things worse for you'.

It seems inevitable that social workers will often have an uphill struggle when their role makes 'confidentiality' very hard to deliver; and where the adults involved may perceive the social worker negatively if they feel criticised as a parent. However, there are things they can do to facilitate the best opportunity for children to engage with them. In Butler and Williamson's (1994) study they highlighted the importance of social workers being perceived by children and young people as listening, that is, through social workers conveying their understanding, checking out what they thought with children and actively engaging them in making choices. All of these things meant that the social workers were more likely to be responded to positively, as was bringing creativity, flexibility and humour to the relationship. Children and young people gave clear messages that they wanted the following from social workers: listening, availability, non-judgemental and non-directive support, humour, straight talking, trust and confidentiality.

Given the wide-ranging role of the social worker involved with a family, particularly if they are also heavily involved with all family members and in legal proceedings, it needs to be acknowledged that inevitably the social worker's knowledge of how the child experiences and views things will be partial and based on information that only represents the child at one point in time. This is not a criticism, but often a reality and, if the analysis of a child's situation and needs is to be fair and balanced, this needs to be acknowledged and of course addressed as far as possible. Consulting widely with others who know the child well; observing the child and receiving information on others' observations in a wide variety of settings over time; doing all that one possibly can to find out about the child; and trying to ensure they do have someone trustworthy and accessible to express their views to, can all help to address the partiality of the picture we have of the child.

However, all too often, social workers fail to acknowledge the limitations of their knowledge about what is happening in families generally and, in particular, with regard to the views of the child. This was often borne out in the Putting analysis into assessment project when assessment reports were read out, either generally or for audit. It was often unclear in the reports to what extent the author had got to know the child; and what level of contact with, and knowledge of, the child the comments were based upon. The evidence regarding the situation of the child and their family and about the quality of parenting itself was often very descriptive and spoke for itself, but there was less clarity when it came to representing children.

Whilst there was usually some attempt to describe children's views, either through what they had said or their presenting behaviour, it was often hard to put this into context. Many of the reports would have benefited from some further discussion of the extent to which the child's views had been elicited so far. In contrast, parents views and perceptions usually made up the main body of the reports.

Sally Holland in her book *Child and Family Assessment in Social Work Practice* (2004) describes similar findings in the study she conducted between 1997 and 2001. She closely examined casework within two neighbouring coastal cities and found that much of the focus in assessments was on establishing the 'verbal performance and ability to provide plausible explanations' for the family problems of parents. Whilst this is necessary, children tended to be excluded or marginalised. Where children were described they were often 'minor characters' in the narrative of assessments, whilst parents were portrayed in a lively in-depth manner. For example in one 25-page report, there were 8 pages of detailed description and analysis of the mother whereas the four children were portrayed in just 2 pages in total, the two-year-old in four sentences. This balancing of the information was not unusual. It was not just the quantity of information about children that was lacking, but the way in which they were described was often two-dimensional and partial.

So why is it so difficult for practitioners to do justice to the contribution children can make to the assessment? Apart from the difficulties in building the relationships with children – and the very real challenge due to their age, verbal and reasoning skills of finding out what they feel, want and have experienced – there is often ambivalence amongst social workers and others involved in assessment regarding how to make sense of and weight the information that children give. In the Putting analysis into assessment project, social workers spoke of the pressure they felt to be 'concrete'. They often did not feel sufficiently well-placed to make clear statements about the meanings of children's behaviour or what they said. There were often fairly general comments about attachment or a child's level of development in relation to what could be expected, but social workers told us that they worried about making these connections in too forthright a manner because they were not psychologists and they expected to be challenged by 'experts' in the court arena. In one local authority we worked with, the legal department discouraged social workers from referring to research and theory in their assessments for this reason. Holland (2004) noted in her study that social work assessments often referred in some way to the child's attachment; but that it was not explored usefully by putting it into context as to how the child was with people other than their parent, for example, or in other settings. She also found an overemphasis on comparing children to developmental norms, in some cases in an unhelpful and unbalanced way. This often resulted in objectifying children and, in some cases, children's names were inserted into text that replicated the language of development charts exactly. The following is one of Holland's examples of this.

> Aran knows and immediately turns to his own name and babbles loudly and
> incessantly and imitates adults' playful vocalisation with gleeful enthusiasm.

The use of evidence, research and theories – such as relating what is known to attachment theory or child development theories – is encouraged, and the Framework for Assessment of

Children in Need and their Families (2000) is grounded in such knowledge, but references to it need to be clear and illustrative. Most importantly, Holland urges, we need to be 'thoughtful and critical' in our application of such knowledge given the potential for 'powerful arguments to be made by using a flawed or overly narrow evidence base'.

Another tendency reported by Holland (2004), and also experienced during the Putting analysis into assessment project, is to influence the reader's thinking about the child through the use of language. For example, if in the same sentence as saying that 'Charlotte has a vivid imagination and seems to take pleasure in getting her friends into trouble' we say that she has told us that she is being bullied, we are undermining what she has told us in quite an obvious way. Or similarly, if we are reporting that a child has been saying she misses her mother (as she is in foster care) but at the same time we say that the child says things only to please her mother, once again we are calling the child's view into question. It is fine to say all of the above things if we can illustrate them clearly with examples – but the ordering of points, the decisions about what we include and what we leave out of a report (verbal or written) are potentially loaded by our motivations in 'arguing a case' with an intended response in mind.

The challenge of representing children accurately and fairly is often increased when working with disabled children, or those whose verbal or non-verbal communication is not readily understood. It is of course essential to draw on all possible resources, creative communication techniques and equipment or facilitators where this may further our ability to ascertain a child's contribution to the assessment, but equally important is the need for the practitioner to acknowledge the gaps and limitations in their understanding. This makes them less likely to misrepresent a child through assumptions or partial information and more likely to identify where the child needs further opportunities to express their views.

And finally, it is crucial to remember that the most important thing to try and understand about and for the children and young people is how they are interpreting the things they are experiencing. Butler and Williamson (1994) highlighted the importance of not just knowing what a child's experiences were, but of understanding the meaning they attached to them. They cite an example of a girl whose father murdered her mother. For her, the fact of the murder was not what she identified as her worst experience, but the lack of communication and support that followed it. The authors found this to be the case with a vast range of experiences – ranging from the extreme to the 'everyday', such as arguments with siblings over a computer game – it was the meaning of the event that mattered. Similarly Holland (2004) cites Scott (1998) as finding, in an Australian study of assessments involving sexual abuse, that much of the focus tended to be on whether or not the case should be labelled as abuse; with assumptions being made about the child's feelings rather than exploring the key issue of 'how is the child?'

During the Putting analysis into assessment project, an analysis tool on this subject was not used. However, the project did generate sufficient information – from exploring themes, reading reports and highlighting key issues – for a checklist to be compiled to assist practitioners and managers when considering the information they have in relation to a child. It can be usefully integrated into the practitioner's analysis.

PRACTICE TOOL: CHECKLIST FOR INVOLVING CHILDREN IN ASSESSMENT

1. **How well do you know the child and to what extent do you know their views, feelings and wishes?** This includes describing your relationship with them, how you think they perceive you, how often you have seen them and in what context – where and who else was present.

2. **Which adults [including professional(s)] know the child best** (what is their relationship like, i.e. how well-placed are they to represent the child's views); **and what do they think the child's key concerns and views are?**

3. **What opportunities does the child have to express their views to trusted or 'safe' adults?** Does the child know how to access people, what would be the barriers and what has been done to ensure they know where to go if they want to talk to someone?

4. **How (if at all) has the child defined the problems in their family/life and the effects the problems are having on them?** This includes the child's perceptions and fears; and what they themselves perceive as the primary causes of pain, distress and fear. What opportunities has the child had to explore them?

5. **When the child has shared information, views or feelings, in what circumstances has this occurred and what if anything did they want to happen?** This should only be stated if known, i.e. can be clearly demonstrated. Assumptions should not be made about a child's motivations for communicating something.

6. **What has been observed regarding the child's way of relating and responding to key adults, such as parents and foster carers? Does this raise concerns about attachment?** This would include describing any differences in the way the child presents with different people or in different contexts. And, where conclusions are being drawn about the child's attachment, the reasons for such conclusions should be clearly demonstrated.

7. **What is your understanding of the research evidence in relation to the experiences this child is thought to have had, and how they might affect them?** i.e. What are the likely or possible impacts on children who experience [*the specific issue at hand, such as parental alcohol misuse, domestic violence*]. This includes a consideration of potential harm along with resilience factors. **How far is what you know of this particular child consistent with the above?**

8. **What communication methods have been employed in seeking the views and feelings of the child; and to what extent have these optimised the child's opportunity to contribute their views?** This includes considerations of whether equipment; facilitators; interpreters; the use of signs or symbols; play; and storybooks could be helpful and whether the child's preferences are known.

9. **How confident are you that you have been able to establish the child's views, wishes and feelings as far as is reasonable and possible for the child?** This would include considerations of things that may have hindered such communication, such as pressure from other adults, time limitations, language barriers or lack of trust in the child–social worker relationship. **How much sense are you able to make of the information you do have?**

CASE STUDY 3.4

Involving children

Kelly	(subject)	8 years old
Susan	(mother)	32 years old
Jim	(father)	31 years old (lives separately but locally)

Kelly has recently come to the attention of social services in the local area. The neighbouring social services were involved with her on two occasions in the past: once in relation to setting up a place in an after-school club for her – this was undertaken by the disabled children's team as Kelly was thought to have mild learning difficulties and behavioural difficulties; and once when a duty visit was undertaken after a neighbour had reported that Kelly had been left home alone. Both parents denied that this had occurred.

Recently, your department has become involved because you have been contacted by Susan's mother requesting help for Susan in managing Kelly's needs. Susan has physical disabilities and is a wheelchair-user; and Jim has recently moved out following an argument with Susan to which the police were called to attend.

A few visits have been undertaken by yourself and other duty social workers since the referral was made and, on these visits, it has been observed that the hygiene levels in the home are poor. The kitchen, lounge and Kelly's room are fairly tidy but in need of a clean and you are aware that Susan's mother visited days ago and said she had cleared up, but Susan's bedroom is very dirty, with beer cans, dirty tissue, used sanitary wear and dirty laundry littering the floor and under the bed. Susan says that Jim was drinking a lot before he left the home and stopped cleaning up a long time ago. Susan is tearful when you meet with her and acknowledges the problems but only when they are pointed out to her.

Carers have been going into the home to help with practical tasks recently and they have raised concerns with their supervisor about what one carer described as Kelly's 'wild' behaviour. She kicks and screams if she doesn't get her own way and tells them she will call the police on them and 'get them arrested for child abuse' when they try and supervise her. Susan is eager to keep Kelly at home and is passive and fairly unresponsive when the concerns about Kelly are raised with her. She starts telling you and the carers who visit that Jim was sometimes aggressive towards her, that he neglected her and Kelly and drank too much. She says she did not tell anyone before because she didn't want people interfering. Initially she did not want Jim to return to the home, but lately she is tearful and missing him, saying that they have spoken on the phone and she hopes he will return.

Susan's mother has just contacted you to say that she is sure (though Susan is denying it) that Jim moved back in on the previous weekend. Kelly's school are describing her as 'very high' and quite 'destructive' in the past few days but stress that her behaviour has been a concern for a long time and she rarely talks about home.

What conclusions can we draw from Kelly's contribution to this assessment so far? Below are some examples of the sorts of points that could be elicited from the checklist headings in relation to this case scenario.

1) How well do you know the child and to what extent do you know their views, feelings and wishes?	The social worker has only known Kelly for a few weeks and seen her, so far, on two occasions. At this stage only an initial assessment has been completed and whilst the social worker has a sense of how Kelly presents in school, after-school club and with her mother, there is a need to more fully explore her views and wishes. Her recent behaviour would suggest that she is unsettled at the moment.
2) Which adults [including professional(s)] know the child best; and what do they think the child's key concerns and views are?	Whilst the carers in the home have the most recent insight into what has been happening to Kelly of late, they have not been involved for long or consistently and their primary role is to give Susan practical support. Kelly has had a consistently good relationship with her teacher, Mrs Morris; and has told the social worker that she likes Rose, the escort on her school bus. Both Mrs Morris and Rose are concerned that Kelly's behaviour has recently been more erratic than usual and that she is seeking more attention through challenging behaviour, but when she gets it is resistant and hostile. They both think Kelly is feeling anxious and unsettled at the moment although they do not know whether or not she would prefer her Dad to come home. She rarely talks about home usually.
3) What opportunities does the child have to express their views to trusted or 'safe' adults?	Although Kelly has some fairly positive relationships with school staff, the escort, and one helper in particular at the after-school club, she usually sees them in group contexts with several other young people. Recently, because people are aware that Kelly is having a difficult time, her teacher and escort have been trying to give her some one-to-one time, which seems to have calmed her down at the time. Susan has acknowledged that she has been upset and preoccupied recently, but has agreed to try and ensure Kelly knows she can talk to her about how she is feeling.
4) How (if at all) has the child defined the problems in their family/life and the effects the problems are having on them?	At this stage Kelly has not explicitly talked about her situation, except for when her helper at the after-school club enquired (because Kelly was picked up by a carer instead of her dad). About this, Kelly said 'He's gone off in a strop hasn't he?'
5) When the child has shared information, views or feelings, in what circumstances has this occurred and what if anything did they want to happen?	When the social worker tried to talk with Kelly about the fact that her dad has moved out and suggested it must feel different at home, Kelly shrugged and asked 'Is he coming back?' in a fairly flat voice. When the social worker told her she doesn't know, Kelly changed the subject instantly, asking the social worker to go into the garden with her before running off outside to see the neighbours 10-year-old boy.
6) What has been observed regarding the child's way of relating and responding to key adults, such as parents and foster carers? Does this raise concerns about attachment?	In the first visit to the home, Kelly was observed to be extremely active, running around, slamming doors and clambering all over the social worker, even though it was the first time of meeting her. She appeared to pay no attention to Susan's attempts at supervising her and was fairly aggressive towards her; swinging her bag around her head so it hit her mother despite being told to stop, and digging her nails into Susan when Susan tried to stop her running off.
7) What is your understanding of the research evidence in relation to the experiences this child is thought to have had, and how they might affect them? How far is what you know of this particular child consistent with the above?	There has been some suggestion by Susan and also highlighted by the recent police attendance at the home, that Kelly has certainly been present when conflicts have taken place between her parents in the form of heated arguments and has possibly witnessed domestic violence. Also, the beer cans, along with claims by Susan and her mother that Jim was drinking heavily in the months preceding his departure, suggest she has experienced seeing her father (and possibly Susan – according to the neighbour) drunk at home on a number of occasions. Both domestic violence and parental drinking are known to increase the likelihood of children of Kelly's age experiencing anxiety, being drawn into conflicts and taking sides with one parent; and of either internalising their feelings and experiencing anxiety or externalising them and presenting with challenging behaviour.

8) What communication methods have been employed in seeking the views and feelings of the child; and to what extent have these optimised the child's opportunity to contribute their views?	Kelly has good verbal communication skills and, in relation to other areas of her life (e.g. school, friendships), tends to make her feelings known to adults around her. Kelly does seem to become most chatty when engaged in imaginative play and in one-to-one situations. The social worker is planning to make some more time available for doing direct work with Kelly to get to know her better. Other professionals involved are trying to make themselves more accessible.
9) How confident are you that you have been able to establish the child's views, wishes and feelings as far as is reasonable and possible for the child? How much sense are you able to make of the information you do have?	Kelly's views about her situation are unclear, but it is obviously not ideal for her to be looked after by a succession of carers with little consistency; and her behaviour recently may be a reaction to this, as well as to her father's sudden departure from the home. It seems, from what Susan and other professionals have said to the social worker, that Kelly has shown signs of being unsettled for some time and the aggressive and challenging behaviour is not new or unusual for her but is more extreme.

The understanding of her views, wishes and feelings at this stage is only partial. |

Practice development session 6

Involving children

Aim

To remind participants of the importance of being critical and thorough in relation to the information provided to them by and about children and young people in order to ensure balanced and fair analysis in relation to them; and to provide an opportunity to test this out in practice.

Method

Exercise 1

This exercise requires a sufficient number of participants for them to form one or more groups of four.

- Ask each set of four participants to sit in two pairs. Name them **A** and **B** (side-by-side) and the facing pair **C** and **D**, as shown below.

  participant **A**   participant **B**

  participant **C**   participant **D**

- Invite each participant to think of an experience they have had (that they are willing to share, i.e. not too emotive) that was either very scary or very exciting.

- Tell the participants that they will tell their story, in the order you instruct them to, and that they will have three minutes to do so.

- For each group of four, invite participant **A** to tell **C** (who they should be facing) their story. At the same time, invite **B** to tell **D** their story. Stop them after three minutes.

- Now ask **C** to tell **A** their story and **D** to tell **B** theirs. Once again, give them three minutes.

  participant **A**   participant **B**
  ↑↓   ↑↓
  participant **C**   participant **D**

- Ask all the participants to turn their chairs round so that **A** now faces **B**, and **C** now faces **D**.

- Invite **A** to tell **B** the story they just heard from **C**; and invite **C** to tell **D** the story they just heard from **A**. Stop them after three minutes.

- Invite the participants to swap over again, so that **B** can tell **A** the story they heard from **D**; and **D** can tell **C** the story they heard from **B**.

  participant **A**   ⇄   participant **B**

  participant **C**   ⇄   participant **D**

■ Tell **B** and **D** to swap seats.

■ Invite **A** to tell **D** the story they have just heard, which will be **D**'s story being repeated back to them. Likewise, invite **B** to tell **C** the story they have just heard. This should mean everyone at this stage gets three minutes to hear their own story told back to them.

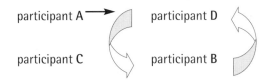

participant **A**   participant **D**

participant **C**   participant **B**

■ Invite participants to quietly reflect on what it was like to have their story told back to them.

■ Ask them, for example: Was it accurate or distorted? Were there key details missing? How did they feel about knowing their story was being told to another when they couldn't listen to what was said? Encourage the participants to draw parallels with the experiences of children giving us information; but stress how diluted and artificial this demonstration is in comparison.

Exercise 2

Presentation

■ Give a presentation on the issues to consider when analysing the information children give us. Use Presentation 5 (see Appendix or download from www.ncb.org.uk/resources/support). Or distribute the section on involving children (pages 60 to 62) for participants to read.

■ Invite discussion on the issues involved.

■ Distribute the checklist for involving children in assessment (page 59) to all the participants.

■ Ask participants to each call to mind a child who they are, or have been, involved with through their work.

■ Invite the participants to form pairs, then proceed according to Option 1 or 2 below.

OPTION 1

■ Encourage the participants, in their pairs, to take it in turns to run through the checklist identifying what significant information they do know about the child and where the gaps are.

■ When they seem to have completed this exercise, ask the pairs in turn to give feedback to the full group on how this went. If necessary, prompt them with questions such as: Did the checklist elicit more information or different information than you might otherwise have provided in an assessment or court report? Do you see any difficulties with either accessing or reporting on some of the information the checklist elicited?

OPTION 2

■ Invite participants to look at one another's reports (you will have asked them to bring a report with them), with the checklist questions in mind.

■ If the participants find there are gaps in the reports, encourage them to tease the information out of each other. Invite them, together, to work out an action plan for establishing a better balance in their understanding of or representation of the child.

Decision theory

In her book *Effective Child Protection* (2002) Eileen Munro explores approaches to decision-making in social work over the last hundred years, commenting that social work has been hampered in building a reliable and consistent evidence base as a result of shifting fashions. Munro explores the potential role of decision theory in social work with children and families.

She states that decision theory rationally portrays people as thoughtful decision-makers, considering alternative actions, deliberating about their consequences; and choosing an option that seems most likely to satisfy goals.

Munro identifies, however, that studies that show how people *actually* reason are striking in the extent to which they show the reluctance of people to make decisions.

In child protection work reluctance to make decisions shows up in a tendency to procrastinate, so that decisions are made in reaction to a crisis rather than a long-term plan. Children in care are particularly vulnerable to failure in active decision-making – and this often results in drift, poor planning and a lack of decisions about contact. According to Munro the same type of drift also shows up in research on child protection, where there is a lack of proactive planning and a tendency to react to crises as they occur. The introduction of timescales is one attempt that has been made towards addressing this problem, which has gone some way towards standardising the practice in the Looked After Children (LAC) system and in assessment.

However, decision-making is a hard task and is both intellectually and emotionally challenging. It can also be hard because decisions often offer imperfect solutions and this can be demoralising. Sharing power is also complex – decisions require a juggling act to give due weight to a range of opinions.

Different schools of thought

Munro highlights two schools of thought that are particularly relevant to thinking about decision-making in social work.

- ■ Decision theorists draw on probability theory and logic to prescribe a model for making decisions.

- ■ Naturalists aim to describe how people actually make decisions.

She suggests that we can draw useful lessons from both schools. While interviewing families, a practitioner will continuously be making many intuitive micro decisions; whereas a decision about whether or not to remove a child from their family will require considerable deliberation and need to be justifiable to the family and legal systems.

Formal decision theory offers a framework for organising reasoning and ensuring that details are not overlooked. Decision theory can help in situations where professionals are feeling confused or overwhelmed by all the factors. Decision theory and more specifically decision trees, which is a formal tool emerging from decision theory, break decisions down into component parts. They are useful in major decision-making when the importance of the subject, for example the well-being of the child, infers significant responsibility on the decider to make the best possible decision. Whilst certainty about the efficacy of a particular decision might be nigh on impossible to reach, it is important to be able to be open and clear and able to demonstrate how decisions were reached.

Decision trees set out a framework for considering possible options; considering the consequences and how probable they are; judging how good or bad those outcomes would be; and picking the option that you believe will have the most beneficial consequence. The framework uses a methodology to decide the **utility value** of decisions made.

Decision trees are an effective way of organising reasoning and analysing the problem. A clear identification of a sequence of events, and the links between them, in itself makes problematic decisions much easier to understand and manage. By making estimates of the probability (likelihood) and desirability of consequences explicit in terms of numbers, it is possible to work out which option has the highest value and show the grounds for the final choice.

Framework for decision trees

1. What decision is to be made?

2. What options are there?

3. What information is needed to help make the choice?

4. What are the likely/possible consequences of each option?

5. How probable is each consequence?

6. What are the pros and cons (desirability) of each consequence?

7. The final decision

The strength of the decision tree is that it makes you think widely. This can also be a disadvantage in that it can generate too much information. Judgement is needed to decide how much effort to put into the decision and therefore how much information to generate. Experience can help the practitioner to reduce the detail to which they need to apply the framework. Hammond (in Munro 2002) suggests applying one's energies to the stages of the decision framework that are most problematic. Quite often when one scans through the whole process it is possible to identify which points can be decided on easily and which ones are the most crucial or difficult for that particular decision.

It is important not to exaggerate the objectivity of decision theory. Although it uses mathematics it is crucial that the practitioner uses their own judgement in giving utility values to the outcomes and assessing their probability, but using the tree does help to push the decision along the analytic–intuitive continuum towards becoming more analytic. It helps break a complicated decision down into smaller and simpler parts. It assists, but does not replace, the human decision-maker.

The decision framework need not be followed in detail in every situation. Professionals can use it to sketch an overview of the decision they are facing and then concentrate on the problematical elements. It encourages people to make their intuitive reasoning explicit and then think it through more thoroughly. It does not remove subjectivity from the process and two rational people will not necessarily reach the same conclusions. It does help to identify where and why they would disagree however, and also provides a clear and defensible account of how a decision was reached, something which may be especially helpful in the current climate.

PRACTICE TOOL: DECISION TREE

Instructions for completing a decision tree.

Read these instructions alongside the decision tree illustration (page 68).

1. What is the decision to be made? Enter data into square on left of tree.

2. What are the possible choices (options)? Enter up to four different options. Write these along the radiating lines coming out of the square.

3. What are the possible consequences of the different options? Create the same number of consequences for each option (3 or 4) and write them along the lines radiating from the circles.

4. Try and give a score to the probability (likelihood) of each consequence occurring. Score somewhere between 0% and 100% (0% = certainly not and 100% = certainly will). The total score across the consequences for one option should equal 100%. You will be likely to use research evidence, practice experience, and discussion and debate to help you decide on this. Place the score in the triangle.

5. Try and decide on the desirability of each consequence occurring. Ascribe a score from 0–10 (0 = least desirable, 10 = totally desirable). These do not need to total up to 10. You have to use your judgement to decide on the desirability: by weighing up the impact on the child, their family, the wider society, cost to agency, etc. Place this score in the last box on the right.

6. Multiply each probability score by each desirability score, and then add these together for each option. This gives you a total score for each option. Place this score in the square inside the tree. The option with the *highest overall score* should be the best option for you to choose as it combines realistic likelihood of success with best desirability.

Decision tree

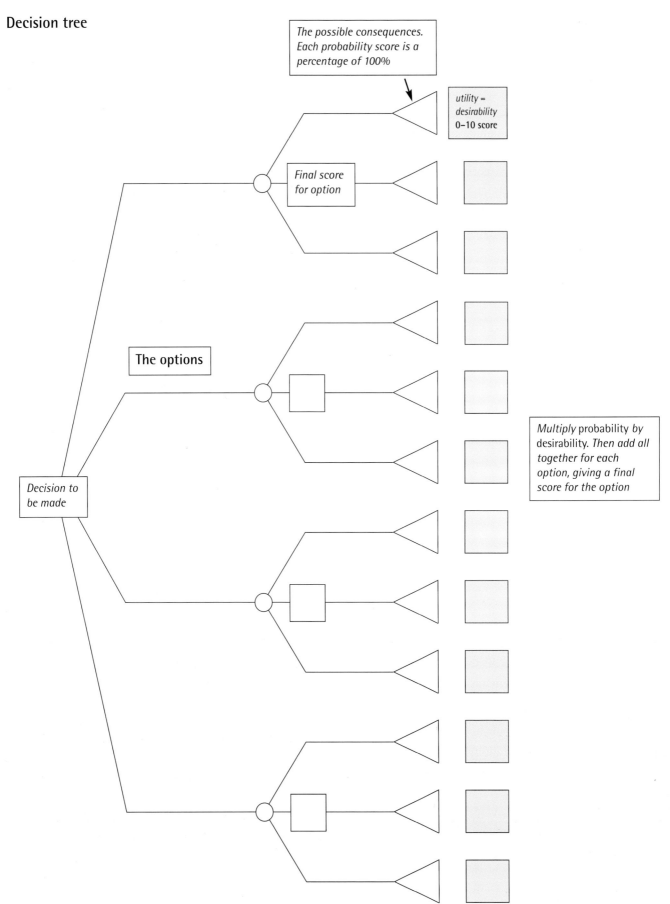

Taken from Eileen Munro (2002) 'Decision Tree', *Effective Child Protection*. Sage Publications.

CASE STUDY 3.5

Decision tree

Family composition				
Name	Gender	Ethnicity	Age	Relationship
Sheila White [nee Philips]	female	White British	45	mother of Paul
Gerald White	male	White British	50	father of Paul
Paul White	male	White British	8	subject (child)
Nancy Philips	female	White British	70	maternal grandmother to Paul

Paul White is the only child of Gerald and Sheila White. Gerald and Sheila married when Gerald was 40 and Sheila 35. Gerald had been in the Royal Marines, Sheila in the WRAF. They met while on active service and left the services and married in 1996.

Both Gerald and Sheila had problems with excessive alcohol consumption whilst in the forces. Gerald had been referred for treatment on two separate occasions prior to his discharge and he narrowly avoided dishonourable discharge.

Sheila had been a very heavy drinker leading to some health problems but it was not until they set up their own home and Sheila became pregnant with Paul that her difficulties came to the attention of health services.

Paul was born one month prematurely and was underweight. He was diagnosed as having mild foetal alcohol syndrome, which left him with some mild facial abnormalities and poor muscle tone.

Physically, Paul has few physical problems now, apart from poor coordination, but his emotional and behavioural development has continued to cause concern.

A special needs assessment was triggered by the nursery that Paul attended from the age of three, because of his flat, unresponsive and withdrawn manner and because he seemed to be exhibiting some developmental delay. Although he has attended mainstream school since he was five, he now has a special needs statement and receives some extra support in school.

The White family have been known to Social Services since Paul's birth.

An assessment was undertaken at the time of his birth (not using the assessment framework) but, as Sheila appeared to be seeking help and attended a support programme through the local alcohol service, no other services were offered.

The school Paul attends has expressed concern to Social Services about the care given to Paul by his parents at times when their drinking was getting out of control on two occasions in the past two years. They felt that he was possibly getting himself up and ready for school and walking to school in the morning, often arriving seeming very tired and hungry. Several reports by neighbours about fighting and neglect have also been received around these times.

An initial assessment was undertaken on the first occasion; but Paul went to stay with his maternal grandmother round the corner for a few weeks, until Sheila got some help and managed to get her drinking under control, and the case was closed. Sheila always seemed to want to work with the school and other agencies to address her son's needs but usually after a reasonable start, matters would deteriorate again.

Paul spoke at the time of wanting to stay with his mummy and daddy but he also told his teacher that daddy was poorly and needed to sleep on the sofa.

Two months ago, the school made a referral in partnership with Paul's maternal grandmother, Nancy. The situation in the family home had deteriorated significantly.

Gerald had been drinking extremely heavily for months and was experiencing severe health problems. He had been admitted to hospital at the weekend suffering from suspected liver failure. He had accepted that he needed help and was saying currently that he was willing to cooperate with health services.

Sheila had also been drinking heavily, albeit more sporadically. According to Paul's grandmother the material conditions in the home were dreadful, with Paul sleeping in soiled sheets and there not being any food in the house. Also, according to Nancy there had been regular fights between Sheila and Gerald.

Paul had continued to attend school fairly well but all the previous week had arrived late, alone and hungry, and had fallen asleep in class several times. He has seemed sad and withdrawn, according to his classroom teacher.

On this occasion, after an initial assessment, a strategy discussion was triggered and agreement reached to proceed with enquiries under Section 47 of the Children Act. A core assessment began and a child protection conference was subsequently convened. Even though Sheila seemed to want to work in partnership with the department, the continuing risk of significant harm to Paul seemed to merit this course of action.

An initial child protection conference was held and Paul was registered on the Child Protection Register under the category of neglect.

A social worker, Ellen Grey, was allocated to the case and she completed a core assessment. Paul went to stay with Nancy, his grandmother, again for a few weeks with his mother's agreement. The assessment had gone well and was nearing completion.

It looked likely that some kind of shared care arrangement between Sheila and Gerald and Nancy would be agreed. Paul would stay with his grandmother with a gradual return home monitored by the core group. An agreement about Nancy taking over his care during stressful periods was reached. A range of supportive services was put in place. Both parents were doing well and had cooperated fully throughout the assessment.

Two days ago, a distraught Nancy phoned to say that Sheila had been found dead that morning at home and it was thought she had died from asphyxiation due to alcohol consumption (commonly known as choking on one's own vomit).

Nancy felt that, although she was willing to carry on looking after Paul in the short term, she was worried about being able to manage everything she needed to do for him on her own on a permanent basis and also it was costing her a fortune.

Sheila's death has thrown the original plan into disarray. Ellen has to make some pressing decisions about Paul's placement, both in the short and longer term. An updated assessment will be required but urgent decisions need to be made in the meantime.

Ellen is torn between leaving Paul with his grandmother – as she feels that this is placing great stress on her (particularly at this sad time after her daughter's death) – and placing Paul with foster carers. She feels that Nancy is well intentioned in wanting to care for her grandson but is concerned about her age and health (she suffers from bronchitis and smokes heavily) and whether she will be able to meet Paul's needs in the longer term. Gerald is overwhelmed by grief and saying that he is going to change and do the right thing by his son. He wants Paul to come home to him. Ellen feels very pessimistic about Paul returning to his father in any permanent way given his past history of relapse.

Paul has been settled at his grandmother's. He has been more alert and responsive at school and seemed happier in himself while living there according to his class teacher.

Ellen decided to complete a decision tree in partnership with her colleague from the family support team who is also in the core group.

They decide to undertake the exercise in order to help them in their thinking about immediate plans for Paul and for the recommendations they will be making to the child protection review conference. The scores given in the decision tree do not indicate the 'right' decision but simply represent the colleagues' thinking about the likelihood and desirability of the various options. Ellen will be better able to explain her decisions and recommendations if she is able to understand her thinking and think through the options with a colleague.

1. The decision to be made is: Where will Paul live? Ellen thinks that care proceedings may need to be instigated for Paul, so that a decision about his future can be made properly – but decisions made about his immediate placement will have implications for the future.

Ellen has to make some quick decisions in partnership with colleagues and with Nancy and Gerald about whether to leave Paul in Nancy's care in the short term; but she also has to think ahead about whether there is any possibility of Paul remaining with Nancy in the long term and, indeed, if this would represent a good plan for Paul.

The options as far as Ellen can see them are as follows.

Option A Paul stays with Nancy with a view to carrying out a kinship assessment to see if Paul's needs will best be met by Paul remaining with Nancy in the long term.

Option B Paul moves to short-term foster carers with a view to seeking and assessing permanent new carers for him, possibly through adoption.

Option C Paul stays with Nancy in the short term but with a view to a permanent new family being sought for him, possibly through adoption.

Option D Paul returns to his father's care with a view to this being a permanent arrangement.

Options A to D are now explored in more detail below.

Option A

This is the option that Ellen favours instinctively. She also knows that The Children Act (s23, para 2) encourages wider use of extended family placements. She believes that this option is likely to be the one with the best outcome. Nancy has a good and affectionate relationship with Paul and he is attached to her. Nancy has helped out in Paul's care for significant periods in the past. Although Ellen has some concerns about Nancy's ability to meet aspects of Paul's needs, such as when he grows into adolescence and some of his educational needs, she feels that a good kinship assessment would identify these areas with Nancy and a plan could be put in place to address these issues.

Ellen has spoken with Paul and he has indicated that he wishes to stay with his grandmother. She feels that this option would be least disruptive for Paul and it would enable him to have an ongoing relationship with his father – who, although Ellen feels is not able to provide satisfactory care for Paul, still has an affectionate relationship with him. Ellen is mindful too of messages from research which (although there is limited evidence from UK research to date) suggest that kinship care is a viable option for long-term care for children, particularly where there is a desire for continued parental contact. Broad and others (2001) in an in-depth study of kinship care in one London Borough, found a significant pattern of 'mid- to long-term stability', which Broad (2004) argues:

> suggests that kinship care goes some way to fulfilling the UK's key child welfare policy aims of reducing the number of placement moves for children looked after, improving placement stability and a child's sense of emotional permanence.

Many of the negative indicators for kinship care relate to poverty, lack of support and training but Ellen feels that there is good support available for kinship carers within her department.

Ellen and her colleague identify three possible consequences of this placement and give a high score to the likelihood of the placement being successful.

Option B

Ellen knows that there are some arguments for a decisive approach to permanency planning, recognising that Nancy is under stress and grieving and will not be in a position to meet Paul's immediate needs and that, in the longer term, it might be better to look at all Paul's needs and seek a family who can meet them all. With this model, Nancy could be considered as a prospective permanent carer if she wished. In theory, short-term carers would be able to assist in the process of assessing Paul's needs and preparing him for permanent placement. Ellen knows that the available research tends to suggest that outcomes for children placed in successful adoptive placements are good, although this is tempered by the difficulties of finding adoptive parents as children (especially boys) get older or if they have special needs. She also knows that contact with birth and extended family is less likely to survive if children are placed for adoption.

Ellen's experience of placing children within her own authority lead her to feel that the chances of a good match with Paul for short-term carers is chancy at best; and that the likelihood of recruiting suitable permanent carers within a reasonable time period is low. Ellen doesn't feel that the placement is 'highly likely' to break down but thinks it is a possibility. She feels pessimistic about the chances of this option leading to a successful transition to a permanent new family; and thinks the likelihood of the short-term placement drifting into a long-term one is high. She therefore scores the consequences accordingly.

Option C

Ellen does not favour this option – of leaving Paul with Nancy in the short term with a view to seeking alternative permanent carers – as she believes this option would be stressful all round. She scores highly the likelihood of a permanent new family not being found and the placement drifting into permanence in an unplanned way. This would mean that the proper kinship assessment would be unlikely to be carried out; and a proper plan to identify Paul's needs and Nancy's capacity to meet them, and the support required to bring this about, would also not be made.

Option D

Ellen is pessimistic about Paul returning to live with his father. Gerald has had significant problems with alcohol over a long period. Sheila was the main carer for Paul and it was only though her efforts that any stability existed, at times, in the family home. Gerald's medical prognosis is poor. He is likely to die if he does not give up drinking but there is no suggestion, based on previous experience, that he would have success in giving up alcohol. Ellen feels that Paul is wary around his father and, although he is pleased to see him for short periods, always seems happy to return to Nancy afterwards. Ellen scores the likelihood of placement breakdown highly and feels that, even if the placement could be maintained, it would be erratic and problematic and would be unlikely to meet Paul's needs.

Scoring the options

Once the likelihood scores are all recorded, Ellen and her colleague place the desirability scores next to each of the consequences. These are largely based on their practice values and experience. Once the calculations have been made, the option that emerges as the most favourable is the option of Paul staying with Nancy whilst a kinship assessment for prospective permanent care is carried out (Option A).

The fact that this option 'won out' may not come as a great surprise. One might ask: what is the point of undertaking an exercise which identifies the option that was favoured in the first place? But carrying out the process has forced Ellen to weigh up the options; discuss them with a colleague; think through the research evidence; and balance this with her knowledge of the child and family and normal practice within her own authority. It has offered her the opportunity to take a step back and come up with considered recommendations. It might prevent a knee-jerk reaction to the catastrophe that has occurred within the family; and this process will enable her to articulate her thinking to various stakeholders. This process does not replace the normal decision-making process within the local authority. If Paul is received into the care of the local authority, the normal Looked After Children decision-making process will take place – but having done the exercise will help Ellen to argue for her chosen option by explaining why she favours one option over others.

Decision tree: Paul

Paul to stay with Nancy permanently (kinship assessment)

(720)

- Paul thrives, successful placement — 70% — 10
- Placement breaks down — 20% — 0
- Placement maintained, poor quality — 10% — 2

Paul to be placed with short-term foster carers – Seek permanent new family (adoption)

(340)

- Successful transition to permanent carers — 20% — 8
- Breaks down, returns to Nancy — 50% — 3
- Drifts as permanent family not found — 30% — 1

Where should Paul live?

Paul to stay short-term with Nancy while permanent carers found

(360)

- Successful transition to permanent carers — 20% — 9
- Paul stays with Nancy by default — 60% — 3
- Breakdown of placement — 20% — 0

Paul returns to father's care with family support

(50)

- Placement successful — 5% — 10
- Placement breakdown — 70% — 0
- Poor (erratic) placement — 25% — 0

Putting Analysis into Assessment

Practice development session 7

Decision tree

Aims

To explore the application of decision theory, including the decision tree, to decision-making with children and families; and to test out this approach in relation to participants' own practice.

Method

■ Introduce the ideas about decision theory using Presentation 1, slides 16 and 17 (see Appendix or download from www.ncb.org.uk/resources/support) and the notes on Decision Theory and Different Schools of thought (pages 65–66).

   Note: If the group has not already covered the intuitive–analytical debate in an earlier session, then include some of the material on Intuition and Analysis (pages 12–13) and some of the earlier content from Presentation 1 here.

■ Ask participants the following questions.

   – How do these ideas relate to your own experiences of making decisions with children and families, particularly during assessment?

   – How would you describe your own decision-making processes?

   – Does anyone here use tools or a specific approach?

   – Would you be interested in a tool that would help you become more analytical and structured in your approach?

Introduce the decision tree, using the following steps.

■ Use the notes in the section above to explain the purpose and potential uses of decision trees. Distribute the blank decision tree and instructions (page 68).

■ Use a case study (such as Case study 3.5, page 69) to talk through how a tree may be completed. It would be useful to run through a previously completed tree (such as the one in Case study 3.5).

■ Invite participants to form groups with no more than six per group.

■ Ask participants in each group to volunteer cases where a crucial decision needs to be made or has recently been made. Then invite each group to agree on which one to use for this exercise.

■ Invite each group to work together on the completion of a decision tree for the case they have chosen. Tell them that they will have 20–30 minutes to complete it.

■ Reconvene the full group, but tell the participants to sit with the members of their small groups.

■ Invite the small groups to give brief feedback to the full group on: the decision that was under consideration; the options considered; the possible consequences; and how (or whether) they reached a decision and agreement on the option that provided the most desirable outcome.

■ Ask the small groups whether they reached consensus easily; what factors they took into consideration when weighing up options; and how much they drew on research evidence, practice experience and so on.

■ Ask the small groups whether they made the decision they think they *would* have made if they had not used this method and, if so, whether doing the exercise using the decision tree would help in explaining or justifying their decision.

■ Ask participants to consider what potential uses the decision tree might have. Answers could include, for example, training, supervision, and providing justification for decisions to managers.

Assessing the impact of parental substance misuse

Issues to consider for analysis

For the purposes of this section we are concentrating on substance misuse in a broad sense but not including alcohol misuse. This is because, whilst many similarities can be drawn there are also significant differences between the two, with regard to their prevalence, 'social acceptability', legality and also the level of knowledge available regarding their potential impact on children's development.

In referring to substance misuse we are referring to 'problem drug use' as defined in *Hidden Harm*, the report by the Advisory Council on the Misuse of Drugs (Home Office 2003), *where problem use is defined as that:*

> with serious negative consequences of a physical, psychological, social and interpersonal, financial or legal nature for users and those around them.

In recent years social workers have become increasingly involved in assessing the needs of, and risks of harm to, children whose parents misuse substances. According to *Hidden Harm*, 200–300,000 children in England and Wales are known to be affected at the current time. Data taken, from 1996–2000, of those accessing services in relation to drug use almost doubled year on year during this time span, which suggests a continued increase in prevalence. Whilst there are varying rates in different geographical areas in the UK, on average one in four of the cases of children on the Child Protection Register are thought to involve parental substance misuse.

The prognosis for children in these families is frequently poor; not just in terms of the potential impacts on them within the home which will be discussed shortly, but in the outcomes of social work intervention, with children's chances of being removed from their parents' care significantly increased. According to *Hidden Harm* (Home Office 2003) less than half of the parents with serious drug problems have their children living with them. When children do remain in their families, social services only tend to become involved when the situation has deteriorated to crisis point, by which time the focus of the work is on protecting children from the worst consequences of their parents' drug use rather than helping the parent address their difficulties (Tunnard 2002a).

Therefore it is hugely important that social workers and the services they work within are geared up to meet the challenge of undertaking good quality assessments, which means they need the knowledge, skills and support to do so.

Substance misuse is an emotive issue. The current emphasis by politicians and in the media on 'tackling drugs' predominantly as a crime issue is likely to influence us all in some way and elicit a reaction; so most people will have some preconceptions or strongly held views of one kind or another about this. In the same way that substance use can be volatile and unpredictable in its impact on individuals, its presence within families with vulnerable children naturally leads to anxiety in practitioners about the unpredictability of the child's experiences. Additionally, because a significant proportion of substance misuse is deemed illegal, the stigmatisation and secrecy that surrounds it makes open and useful interventions – in which practitioners and parents can collaborate to resolve the difficulties – unlikely, and very difficult to achieve.

Forrester (in Philips 2004, Chapter 10) stresses the importance of recognising the *impact* of our feelings and values in relation to substance misuse before we can respond openly and effectively to it. He puts forward the following Four assessment principles to assist in focusing our assessments of children's needs when there is parental substance misuse.

Four assessment principles

1. Maintain a focus on the child. Collecting information regarding the pattern of drug use is of limited utility in making an assessment if all the other variables are not also focused on. How does the substance use impact on the child? How is the child progressing and understanding any reasons for the difficulties they may have?

2. An adult's management of their own life can be a good indicator of their ability to look after a child (the measure being whether the parent is causing themselves harm through a failure to manage their own life).

3. Past behaviour is the best predictor of future behaviour. A good chronology and full social history, which is best completed by involving the parent and child (if appropriate) can greatly assist this.

4. A variety of sources should be used for information, including different agencies and the wider family. For example, grandparents are often a valuable source of information and support.

(Adapted from Donald Forrester 'Social work assessments with parents who misuse drugs or alcohol', in Phillips (2004) *Children Exposed to Parental Substance Misuse: Implications for family placement*, pp. 172–4.

So what do we know about the impact of parental substance misuse on children? So much of course depends on the nature of the substance misuse. It is not possible to address in detail here all the potential variables that come into play, except to highlight that there are many and to be wary of generalisations.

The evidence is still only partial as well, with the absence of many longitudinal studies demonstrating the impact on young people's development over time. Some useful sources of information regarding this issue are listed in the bibliography at the end of this toolkit. It is not possible to provide detailed discussion here about the research and evidence in this area, but below are just some of the things we do know.

Children of substance-misusing parents are more likely to experience neglect and emotional abuse (but not necessarily other forms of abuse) than other children. Their daily lives are often unpredictable and characterised by separations (short- and long-term) from their parents, siblings or wider family. Also, families can become isolated, increasing the child's vulnerability in these circumstances because, as Cleaver and others (1999 p.41) puts it:

> bizarre or unpredictable behaviours can alienate friends and family; families wish to hide their experiences; friends and social activities are based around parent's current needs and circumstances.

Children may also, within this context, be undertaking caring responsibilities for their parent or siblings or an inappropriate level of self-care; and if, as is often the case, they are afraid to discuss this for fear that professionals will judge their parents or break up the family, they may not get any practical or emotional support with this.

In terms of the risk factors associated with serious injury to children, Forrester (2004) points to: the presence of young babies where it is indicated that the parent is having problems caring for the child or themselves, families where there are high levels of repeated violence (particularly if alcohol misuse is involved) and where there is a dual diagnosis of substance misuse and mental illness (particularly when this is associated with violence).

In her review of impact and intervention studies, Tunnard (2002a) reported that the following factors mitigated some of the harm to children in most studies: where parents planned some separations, such as sending children to stay with grandparents as a way of protecting them from their drug use; and when parents had protective strategies of some kind, such as safe storage of equipment, keeping other drug users out of the home or having rules about not using drugs when the children were around. Also, when parents went into treatment and in particular if they switched from heroin to methadone, this often brought notably increased stability, better standards of care and a release from secretiveness and the pursuit of money and drugs.

Pregnancy and/or having a baby (with or without their own opiate withdrawal symptoms) can also be strong motivators for change. When parents are motivated it is vitally important that they can easily access the support they need and that this motivation isn't crushed through others' (including professionals') lack of belief in them. However, it can be problematic to reduce usage too quickly in pregnancy and better if this is supported in a planned way.

Prior to the birth of babies of parents with problem substance misuse, it is important to consider and carry out pre-birth assessments. Indicators such as a failure to seek antenatal care by parents with mental illness (defined as including substance misuse) have been correlated with incidents of fatal child abuse (Reder and Duncan 1999). So whilst there can be a fear of undermining any future ability to engage with parents by proactively assessing the needs and risks of harm to their babies prior to birth:

> our wish to respond to the real difficulties of parents and to give them every opportunity to bring up their children must not distract us from the needs of the baby.
>
> (Hart, 2000 in Horwarth 2001, Chapter 15)

The role of partners is crucially important in relation to substance misuse. Parental tension, conflict and in many cases domestic violence are common, but where a partner is a non-drug user and supportive of their partner's commitment to reduce or cease drug use, this has been seen to lead to better outcomes and to benefit children.

The impact of different drugs on individuals, and in turn on their parenting, is impossible to predict or generalise and it is vitally important that professionals seek out information to fill in their knowledge gaps about potential impacts, whilst recognising the complex range of individual factors at play. However there are indicators of some trends in how certain drugs can affect parental behaviour. For example, amphetamines can be associated with aggression, as can, according to anecdotal reports, the use of crack cocaine. These reports go on to say that crack cocaine users therefore, when experiencing the 'come down', often take other drugs such as cannabis to counter feelings of agitation and to calm them.

It should not be assumed that parental substance misuse automatically means parents are unable to care adequately for their children, nor that achieving total abstinence as soon as possible is always the most sensible and desired outcome. Indeed if parents do cease to use drugs it may not address the problems they have with parenting and may result in other issues being identified, such as depression previously masked by drug use. What is important is seeking to understand as far as possible the parents' position, perception, goals and fears, whilst not losing sight of the risks to the child, which need to be looked at in a specific and illustrative way.

We should not underestimate the fears (real and valid) that parents have about acknowledging their substance misuse. Addiction is highly associated with denial and minimisation; and dealing with this can be very challenging and feel like it leads to a dead-end for the social worker trying to engage with a parent. However, it is useful to consider critically to what extent our practices are unintentionally reinforcing such denial. Miller and Rollnick (2001) argue that 'denial is not inherent, but a product of a confrontational style of interaction' and that good empathic listening, at the heart of the Motivational interviewing approach they put forward, is far more productive.

Practitioners should ask themselves: Do parents feel that they have permission to admit to not being able to cope with parenting unsupported, that they need some support, time and space to concentrate on addressing their drug problems? Or would they be right in thinking such an admission would be seen not as a way forward but as further evidence in a case that is inevitably building against them? Similarly, when practitioners know that parents are struggling with structure and appointment times, are they setting them up to fail by only offering office appointments or ones in the morning for example? Whilst some testing out naturally occurs within the social work relationship and provides useful information, it could also prevent the possibility of securing cooperation within a trusting, constructive relationship, and moving forward. This is not to be mistaken for false optimism or naïve practice. Of course if parents are unable to provide practitioners with explanations or demonstrate a commitment to the assessment process, the practitioners have no choice but to fill in the gaps. And they need to go at a child's pace. It would be wrong to allow a situation to go on for too long while a parent is testing out their capacity to change, which can be a lengthy process, if the child is at risk of harm or unsettled; but it is worth questioning whether practitioners can do more to secure common ground and goals with parents.

It is for all these reasons that this is such a difficult area of work, with no easy answers or formulas. However, knowledge and skills development, the time and space to reflect, and good interagency links and joint working protocols are all important for providing a context for practitioners to maximise the likelihood of completing accurate, timely and forward-looking assessments, as is a thorough, reflective and non-judgemental approach by practitioners.

PRACTICE TOOL

The following form was adapted by J Powell (National Children's Bureau, 2001, unpublished) from the Standing Conference on Drug Abuse (SCODA) guidelines for professionals assessing risk of harm to children when working with drug-using parents. The guidelines have been adapted so that the information is collated under the dimensions of the Framework for Assessment of Children in Need and their Families *(Department of Health and others 2000).*

THE ASSESSMENT OF PARENTS WHO USE DRUGS

Assessment of family functioning and the impact it has on parental capacity

1. **Pattern of parental drug use**
   - Is there a drug-free or supportive partner?
   - Is the drug use stable or chaotic? (i.e. swings between states of intoxication and withdrawal and/or poly-drug use)
   - Is alcohol a part of the repertoire of drug use?
   - Exactly what drugs are used? (ask specific questions, e.g. refer to yesterday or last weekend)
   - How much is spent on an average day or week?
   - Have there been any (voluntary) significant drug-free periods?
   - What is the history of drug use? Is it escalating? Is it a response to specific events or stressful periods?
   - How are the drugs used? (e.g. injected or smoked).
   - What are the behavioural implications? (e.g. inconsistent behaviour, drowsiness or unavailability)

2. **How the drugs are procured**
   - Are the children left alone while the parents are procuring drugs or getting the money to do so?
   - Are the children being taken to places where they could be vulnerable?
   - Where does the money to buy drugs come from?
   - Are the parents frequently arrested? Are there any outstanding criminal offences yet to be dealt with? Are the parents on probation?
   - Is the home used for selling drugs, stolen items or prostitution?
   - Are the parents allowing the home to be used by other drug users?

3. **Health risks**
   - Where are the drugs normally kept? Could children have access to them?
   - If parents are injecting drugs, are needles shared? How are syringes or needles disposed of?
   - Are the parents or children registered with a GP? Is the GP aware of the drug use?
   - Are the children ever given drugs?
   - Do the parents have health problems associated with drug use?

4. **Parents' perception of the situation**
   - Do the parents see their drug use as harmful to themselves or their children?
   - What strategies are used to minimise the impact on the children?
   - Do the parents perceive a difference in their childcare when they are using drugs and when not?

5. Pregnancy

 ■ Was drug use revealed during the pregnancy? At what stage?

 ■ Was the mother in treatment during the pregnancy? If so, were any other drugs used in addition to those prescribed?

 ■ At what gestation period did the mother book for antenatal care?

 ■ If the baby needed hospital treatment for withdrawal symptoms, how did the parents cope during this time? What observations were made of their care and visiting of the baby?

Environmental factors

1. Physical needs/home environment

 ■ Is the accommodation adequate for the children?

 ■ Does the family move frequently?

 ■ Are other drug users sharing the accommodation?

 ■ Can the parents control what happens in the home?

 ■ Is there adequate food, clothing and warmth for the children?

 ■ Have employment and income been affected by parental drug use?

2. Social networks and support

 ■ Do the parents and children associate mainly with other drug users?

 ■ What support is available from extended family and friends? Do they know about the drug use?

 ■ Are the parents in treatment now or have they been in the past? What services have helped in the past?

 ■ Do the parents know what help and resources are available locally? What are the barriers to accessing help?

Children's developmental needs

1. Family and social relationships

 ■ Do the children have contact with other adults outside the family? Is there a consistent, caring adult who can meet their cognitive and emotional needs?

 ■ Do the children have age-appropriate friendships outside the home or are the family stigmatised because of drug use?

2. Emotional and behavioural development

 ■ The older children of drug-using parents can sometimes assume inappropriate parental responsibility. Is this the case? Are they young carers themselves?

 ■ Are the children being left to fend for themselves or look after younger siblings?

 ■ Consider what the children's experience of home life would be. How would they experience their parents' behaviour? Does it concern, frighten or embarrass them?

3. Health

 ■ Are the children registered with a GP and receiving routine health surveillance?

 ■ What information do the children have about substance misuse? Do they know about their parents' drug use?

Name	Age	Ethnicity	Role
George Ford	29	White British	father
Kirsty Penrose	31	White British	mother
Charlotte Ford	10	White British	daughter
Phillip Ford	8	White British	son

Summary

Charlotte and Phillip both live with their father, George, in a three-bedroom council flat in London. Their mother is no longer living with them and they see her only occasionally when she turns up unexpectedly at their school, paternal grandparents' house or the flat. She used heroin and crack cocaine when she was still living mostly in the home (she sometimes used to disappear for days), was increasingly chaotic and unable to manage her care of the children. George used to smoke cannabis and drink but did not use heroin, crack or other drugs; and increasingly took on more and more responsibility for the children. Meanwhile, George and Kirsty argued more and more and when George accused Kirsty of turning to prostitution she stormed out and hasn't been seen since.

This information has been passed on by George's brother-in-law who has phoned social services to report his concern for the children, as he says that now George is a 'druggie' too and unable to look after the children. He is fed up with his wife (George's sister) covering for George and having to go round and look after the children because, he says, George isn't.

George has been to a local needle exchange for support and advice and has spoken to a drug worker about his use recently. Therefore some information is available about his drug usage. Also Phillip talked to his cousin Terry recently, who passed on what he said to his parents, which also prompted the referral. After agency checks and discussions with George and the children, the following information is available in relation to the assessment questions above.

Assessment of family functioning

1. Pattern of drug use

A few months ago, George smoked heroin with some friends at the weekend. He did this occasionally for a few weeks, but gradually his usage crept up into some weekdays and more recently he has begun injecting, often once, but increasingly twice per day.

He has a part-time job as a caretaker in a housing complex in the afternoons, although he has had a couple of warnings lately for turning up late and neglecting some of his duties. He has been paying for the drugs (last week he spent £95) from his wages, but neglecting to pay bills and his rent is going into arrears. Also, George has been borrowing bits of money here and there from friends and his sister and has run up a credit card bill to its £1000 limit.

George told the drug worker that his father (his only remaining parent) died just two weeks before he first used heroin and he is getting quite depressed but trying not to think about things.

2. How drugs are procured

More often than not, George has bought a few days' worth of heroin from his dealer/friend who sometimes comes to George's home in the evening to deliver it, or if not, George goes to his flat nearby in the morning after dropping the children off at school. On two occasions George has left the children for a short while to obtain his drugs, phoning his sister to ask her to go round and look after them, but not waiting until she arrives.

3. Health risks

Currently George is quite run down and he has lost some weight. The reason he went to the needle exchange recently was on the advice of a friend because he thought he was getting an infection in his arm where he was injecting. He has obtained information regarding safer injecting.

4. Parents' perception of the situation

George, when questioned by the social worker about his drug use has not talked in as much detail as he has to the drug worker about it, but has admitted that 'now and then' he uses heroin. He thinks he organises things so that it doesn't impact on the children. He thought they didn't know and was shocked when told that Phillip had told his cousin his dad was 'probably gouched out at home' and on the same occasion Phillip said 'He's a junkie like Mum ain't he?' George thinks that Phillip is probably aware about drugs more because of Kirsty's previous drug use. So far, George's strategy to minimise the impact of his drug use on the children has been to conceal it from them and bring in back-up to help out with them (particularly in the evenings), he has often been asking his sister or female friend Marcia round or arranged for the children to stay with his sister and brother-in-law.

5. Pregnancy:

Not applicable

Environmental factors

1. Physical needs/home environment

The flat is adequate for the family's needs and they have lived there for four years. Recently, the conditions in the home have deteriorated, although George's sister and his daughter Charlotte have been trying to minimise the mess and dirt. Charlotte started washing up and hoovering when her paternal grandfather died because she wanted to support her Dad and hates mess.

Also, the food cupboards and fridge have very little in them lately and George is tending to shop for convenience foods on a daily basis rather than doing a weekly shop, partly because his access to money is dwindling. George has also told his sister he is worried about losing his job if he doesn't 'sort it out'.

2. Social networks and support

George is getting support with the children from his sister and his friend, Marcia. He does associate with some other drug users and knows several through Kirsty, but tends to keep his socialising to outside of the home, although this has been more difficult since he is on his own with the children. George's sister is annoyed with George because he didn't admit to using heroin to her until recently, although she strongly suspected it. She does feel sorry for him though and is worried about the impact on him of their father's death. She also doesn't want the children to come to harm, but has a teenage son of her own and is finding the situation increasingly a strain.

George knows something about treatment and support options because he has learnt about this in the past when trying to support Kirsty.

Children's developmental needs

1. Family and social relationships

The children get on well with their aunt and uncle and occasionally stay for weekends with their maternal grandparents. George has tended to be the most consistent adult in their lives until recently because Kirsty was very erratic in her involvement with and care of them.

Phillip tends to have friendships with older boys (including his teenage cousin) and to be fairly disruptive among his peers at school. Charlotte has been fairly withdrawn for a long time; and is friendly with some children at school and in neighbouring flats but tends to be on the sidelines in their group interactions. She has not talked to other children or adults about either Kirsty's or, more recently, George's drug use; no one is sure to what degree she is aware of it.

Emotional and behavioural development

Recently, Charlotte has been undertaking more and more responsibilities within the home and Phillip is viewing Charlotte increasingly as his responsibility, including supervising her, which he does quite aggressively at times. Charlotte was very tearful and frightened when her dad last left her and Phillip alone (according to her aunt who arrived later) because she didn't know where her dad was and seemed to think he was 'getting into trouble with someone'.

More information is needed about how the children are experiencing home life. Phillip has described the home as a 'shit tip' in an argument with his dad; and has described his dad as 'out of it' to his cousin, although George doesn't agree that Phillip would have seen him like this.

Health

The children are both registered with the GP and do not have any health difficulties currently. Phillip clearly knows about his father's and Kirsty's drug use but it is unclear what Charlotte knows. Nor is it clear what support and accurate information either of them have been given, as George is still keen to conceal the issue from them.

Overall review of the information

If the above case information was to be considered with reference to the Four assessment principles described earlier (page 77), then it would seem that more information is needed regarding the children's progress; that is, a better picture of how they are getting on at school and how they present in different situations with different people. It does seem clear, however, that attention needs to be paid to helping them understand their experiences and to express their feelings and worries, particularly given their history of experiencing chaotic and inconsistent parenting.

George's management of his own life has previously been more adequate as far as is known, but recently he appears to be losing a grip – not just on his job, his health, his finances, the home and his increasingly building heroin use – but also on his ability to recognise the children's needs.

In terms of past behaviour, from what we know, George was the better able of the two parents and more supportive of the children's needs, although he did not manage to curb his cannabis and drinking use consistently (but did for some periods) or to avoid conflicts with Kirsty in front of the children. He has exhibited strengths, insight and has utilised support (for example his sister) in the past; and exploring this with him, if it were possible to engage him honestly in this, could have positive outcomes if he were to regain his focus on the children's needs.

Some of the potential sources of information which would aid the assessment in this case are: the maternal grandparents, Kirsty if her whereabouts became known, the aunt, uncle, cousin, school, GP, drugs worker, and housing department.

Practice development session 8

Substance misuse

Aim

To help practitioners reflect on their assessments of children's needs in families where there is parental substance misuse.

Objectives

■ To enable participants to consider their own drug awareness and to identify whether further training or support in this area would be useful.

■ To identify messages from participants' experience and knowledge of working with families where parents are misusing drugs.

■ To provide information regarding the potential impact on children of parental substance misuse; and to consider these issues in a holistic way, taking into account all aspects of the child's and family's experiences.

■ To consider issues for assessment and to apply a framework ('The assessment of parents who use drugs') adapted from the SCODA guidelines (1987) to a real case.

Methods

There are a number of alternative activities for this session, so selecting the most appropriate ones is the first step.

The sticky note game

a) Distribute pads of sticky notes to the participants. Invite each participant to write the name of a drug (legal or illegal) on a sticky note and place it on someone else's forehead.

b) Tell the participants that they must now go round the group asking questions – to which respondents can only answer yes or no – in order to establish what drug they have on their forehead.

c) If possible, lead on from this activity to a discussion of how confident the participants are about their level of drug awareness and, if they are not confident, to advice about how to address this.

Ideas storm

d) Place three flip chart sheets where all the participants can see them.

e) Write the three Framework for assessment triangle domains, each on a different flip chart sheet.

f) Ask participants to think about the possible impacts on children of living with substance misuse in relation to these headings.

Presentation

g) Use Presentation 6 from Appendix to present factual information.

Use case studies to demonstrate the assessment format

h) Invite participants to form pairs or small groups.

i) Distribute the handout on the assessment of parents who use drugs (page 83).

j) Invite each pair or group to choose a case that they can discuss. If they do not have a suitable one, then give them copies of Case study 3.6 (page 82).

k) Tell them to work through the questions in the assessment of parents who use drugs handout (page 83) and consider what they know in relation to their case. Ask them to consider and give feedback on the following.

   – Would this assessment format help in undertaking this assessment?

   – How would the information be obtained/gathered?

   – How would you work with the adults, children and other family members both to obtain the information and support them in the areas identified?

   – What additional tools might you use?

   – How would you involve other agencies?

   – Are there some areas of information about a family that stand out as being the most important and having an overriding influence on your assessment?

l) Facilitate a discussion with the group in relation to these areas. This should provide useful information, not just about whether utilising the assessment format is useful, but about the difficulties and issues arising for workers. This, in turn, might help identify the need for the provision of further information, training, building of better links with relevant adult services and so on.

m) Participants could work through the Four assessment principles (page 77) with reference to the case they are discussing and consider to what extent these have been adhered to/established in the case work so far and what else can be done to ensure they are.

4. Reviewing and recording decisions

Conclusions and reporting

This toolkit has looked at a number of principles, approaches and tools, all designed to aid analytical thinking in assessments. Clearly, establishing the agency's position and conclusions regarding the needs of children and their families should be an ongoing process of information-gathering; observations; checking out; reflection; consideration of evidence, research and theory as it relates to the case; and more besides. If practice is undertaken in a dynamic, thorough and thoughtful way such as this, it could be and often is hard to know when the assessment can be considered 'finished'.

In the case of assessments undertaken within the *Framework for Assessment of Children in Need and their Families* (Department of Health and others 2000), the timescales that accompany the framework may provide the cut-off point that determines at what stage a report is written up. However, in very many cases, this is merely a 'mark in the sand', a record of where the author of the report was up to in their knowledge and thinking about a family's situation at a particular point in time. This is because often the agency's involvement will continue and the assessment, along with any recommended intervention, is ongoing.

Some of the practitioners involved in the Putting analysis into assessment project commented that they did not feel that they were in a position to draw conclusions, with the level of clarity that was expected of them, after the 35-day time limits were up. It is important that practitioners, and the managers who support them, are willing to acknowledge the limitations of their understanding and knowledge within reports; and to recommend, as appropriate, what further action needs to be taken to address this.

This section will look at some of the important points for practitioners to bear in mind both when reaching conclusions and reporting on them. It will draw on some existing work in this area: namely that of Holland (2004), who also cited Sheppard and others (2001); and that of Raynes (in Calder and Hackett 2003).

So firstly, what does a practitioner need to consider in reaching their conclusions? For their own integrity, they will want their conclusions to be as fair, balanced and accurate as possible. They should therefore be clear that they have a good balance of information and a critical approach to making sense of it. They should have gathered and be ready to present information that both supports and disputes their original, emerging and most recent hypotheses; and include the perspectives of all relevant parties, family members and professionals. Where there are disagreements in perspectives, the practitioner should resist the temptation to use language that undermines one point of view and amplifies another.

It is important and can be helpful to remember that a practitioner's conclusions are theirs alone. They neither have a crystal ball, nor do they know everything there is to know about the past, present or the likely future. The practitioner can, therefore, only seek to provide a well-thought-out weighing up of what they do know; and, if done fairly, honestly, highlighting strengths and weaknesses, avoiding stereotypes, unfair assertions and denigrating language, they should not be able to stray too far from the 'truth' as they know it.

The practitioner's conclusions should draw on a wide view of the family's circumstances, being careful not to overlook or minimise the significance of social and environmental factors, such as people's experience of poverty or discrimination. The practitioner should acknowledge the impact of power imbalances which affect the relationship they have with family members. Holland (2004), citing Sheppard and others (2001) puts forward the following characteristics, which should be features of conclusions.

Conclusions should be forward looking and solution focused. They should give due consideration to answers to the questions: What, from the past, can be built on? What is indicating itself as helpful or protective? What needs to happen to encourage this? To what extent can we find overlap in ours [the practitioner's] and the families' goals and harness this? Conclusions should also be flexible to both the changing circumstances of families and the changing needs of children over time. They should be balanced and integrate the views of service users.

When it comes to the practitioner reporting on their conclusions, it is important and only fair to service users that they provide an account of the decision-making process, explaining what they looked for, weighed up and how they reached the conclusions they did.

The report should of course be placed in context as to why the practitioner is involved; what the level and nature of their involvement with the family has been; and where, when and how many times they have seen the parents, child and so on. They should also refer to who they have consulted. The practitioner should also be explicit about any research that has informed their thinking, and the tools they have used to elicit views and facts, including describing how they have worked with children to involve them in the process.

The importance of the use of language in the report along with the ordering of points should not be underestimated. Even fairly innocuous-seeming words, such as 'claims' when applied to parents, when 'said' or 'stated' is being used for professionals' views, implies a different valuing of the information they are giving. It is important for the practitioner to be conscious of this, particularly given the pressure to 'make a case' in the, unfortunately, often adversarial court arena. Similarly, the practitioner must be careful not to always start with the negative when describing parents or children, which can have the impact of undermining any positives or strengths that are explored later. If negative facts or risks are described fairly, accurately and illustratively, they should speak for themselves and their importance be acknowledged in the final analysis – so their potency will not be reduced by acknowledging the positive things, such as a family's honesty or pro-activeness in seeking their child's return home.

Finally, there should be an acknowledgement that people are not fixed in their behaviour; and an exploration of a parent's capacity for change and the prognosis for desired changes to occur should be explored. Recommendations that result from the assessment should be clearly stated with targets set where applicable, spelling out clearly what changes need to occur and by when.

PRACTICE TOOL: CHECKLIST FOR CONCLUSIONS AND REPORTING

When looking at one's own or others' reported conclusions, it may be useful to have the following questions in mind.

■ Have the views of the relevant family members been established and integrated accurately and fairly?

■ Is the view that is presented balanced; with a weighing up of positive factors, strengths and resilience factors alongside risks of harm and unmet needs?

■ Is it clear how the decision was made? Has the process been made explicit? This includes not only the final decision-making process but also how the assessment was carried out, for example in terms of numbers of visits and who was consulted.

■ Is there anything about the use of language that is unnecessarily loaded or undermining? Are there stereotypes or pathologising language in evidence?

■ To what extent does the ordering of points impact on the way the report is received or understood? Are family members tending to be portrayed at first negatively?

CASE STUDY 4.1

Conclusions and reporting

Name	Age	Ethnicity	Role
Malcolm Bradley	39	White Irish	father
Jenny Bradley	41	White Irish	mother
Selina Bradley	15	White Irish	daughter
Glen Bradley	12	White Irish	son
Beatrice Bradley	3	White Irish	daughter

The school referred the above family to social services originally because they have been worried about Glen. He has been increasingly aggressive and argumentative in school recently. He is a very able child, but seems apathetic and not to be concentrating or applying himself to his work as much as he did until just a few months ago. He has also been bullying younger children.

Malcolm agrees that there has been a deterioration in Glen's behaviour and says that Glen has been very hostile towards him and takes no notice of him most of the time. Malcolm was made redundant 6 months ago and has been drinking fairly regularly in the day and more than usual.

Jenny has had several periods of depression over the years and seems to be exhibiting feelings of paranoia and anxiety recently. When asked about how she was feeling recently she said 'probably like my mum' and stared into space. Malcolm told the social worker that Jenny's mother disappeared when she was three years old and that at the moment she seems quite preoccupied with this.

Selina has moderate learning disabilities and the special school she attends are concerned that she is increasingly exhibiting sexualised behaviour towards male teachers and some pupils. When this was raised gently with Selina she had a giggling fit. Her parents did not seem very worried as they thought it natural for her to be inquisitive about her body and those of others at her age. They did not seem very comfortable about the idea of talking with Selina about sex and said they have avoided doing so up to now.

Beatrice is slightly overweight and a very placid child. Jenny seems very reluctant for anyone to look after Beatrice other than her and is quite anxious about her, often wondering without cause (in the GP's view) if Beatrice has various illnesses or disabilities. The health visitor has been quite concerned about Jenny's anxiety in relation to Beatrice.

Jenny also seems to have become quite obsessive about cleaning recently, repeatedly scrubbing and polishing the same areas within less than an hour of doing it. Jenny does not work and hasn't for several years.

Within practice development session 9 there is an opportunity to develop this case study and to practice forming and wording conclusions that are in line with the principles discussed earlier.

Practice development session 9

Conclusions and reporting

Aim

To reflect on how conclusions are reached, what they should 'look like' and how they are reported on; and to provide participants with an opportunity for peer feedback and to test out ideas in practice.

Methods

Activity 1

■ In advance of the session, you could ask each participant to bring an assessment report (ideally an initial assessment, as a core assessment would take longer to read). Remove any references to the subjects of the reports (i.e. make them anonymous).

■ Mark the reports in a way that will ensure that you do not give the report back to the author for the activity itself. Staple two blank sheets of paper to the back of each report.

■ Give a ten-minute presentation about conclusions and reporting using Presentation 2, slides 12 to 14 (See Appendix or download from www.ncb.org.uk/resources/support).

■ After the presentation, invite questions and discussion of any issues it raises for participants.

■ Invite participants to form pairs.

■ Give out the assessments, trying to ensure that no one gets their own.

■ Ask the pairs to look at each of the assessments. Ask them to look with a (supportively) critical eye and ask themselves the following questions:

   - Is the child visible? Are their needs identified?

   - Is there evidence of theory and research in the assessment?

   - Are the domains and their interrelationship clearly articulated?

   - Is the decision-making process thinking/weighting of issues apparent?

   - Are cultural issues addressed?

   - Is it clear what needs to happen and how change will be measured?

■ Invite each pair of participants to record two points that are positives; and two that are suggestions for how the assessment could have been strengthened – particularly from an analytical perspective. (Making four points in all.)

■ Ask the pairs to pass the assessments on to another pair (still trying to ensure that no one has their own) and repeat the exercise.

■ Collect in the assessments and then pass each to its owner (author).

■ Ask the participants to read all the comments and reflect on them; then to discuss with their partner whether the comments are helpful and might strengthen their future practice.

■ Ask for two or three volunteers to briefly summarise their assessment and read out the comments, stating how the comments might have helped them. Stress that there are lots of reasons for people not being able to do everything that the theory tells them is good practice – so urge people not to feel too defensive.

■ To round off the activity, allow time for participants to share any thoughts that have arisen from receiving such feedback on their report.

Activity 2

■ Divide the group into smaller groups of three or four.

■ Ask each small group to come up with a set of conclusions and recommendations, either for a case that one of them has been working on or (imaginary conclusions) for Case study 4.1 (distributing the case study if necessary).

■ Stress that they should take care to ensure that their conclusions are: forward looking, balanced, flexible to changing circumstances, and that the views of service users are considered and integrated. And also that they consider their use of language and ordering of points.

■ Ascribe different roles to the members of the small group for a role-play exercise. Choose one member of each group to be the social worker or team manager who is going to tell the 'recipient' their conclusions and recommendations, including how they were reached.

■ Choose one or two members of each group to be the recipients of the information. If using the case study, the recipients might be: Jenny, Malcolm, one of the children, the referrer, health visitor, or someone from one of the schools.

■ Decide which member of the group will be the observer. Explain to them that they will watch the role-play and then be asked to give feedback on their observations afterwards.

■ Once roles are assigned and group members have formed a set of conclusions in their minds (notes may be taken), instruct the participants to role-play the social worker or manager giving the information to the agreed participants. Tell them they will have five minutes for this.

■ After five minutes (or longer if you feel it is needed) stop the role-play and invite feedback from those in each role, including observers.

■ If time permits, swap the roles around, changing the recipient's identity, and repeat the role-play.

■ Invite feedback about the role-play, asking to what extent people were able to be forward looking, for example, or to explain the decision-making process.

Critical decision method

This story-based approach was first put forward by Gary Klein (Klein 2000). Klein belongs to the naturalistic school of decision theorists. His approach is to look for what can be learnt from the patterns and stories that emerge from examining a wide range of different decision-making situations. In his book, *Sources of Power: How people make decisions* (2000), he suggests that we organise our cognitive world – the world of ideas, concepts, objects and relationships – by linking the various parts into stories. He proposes that by understanding how this happens, we can learn to make better use of the power of stories.

Klein suggests that a story is a blend of several ingredients:

- **agents** – the people who figure in the story

- **predicament** – the problem the agents are trying to solve

- **intentions** – what the agents plan to do

- **actions** – what the agents do to achieve their intentions

- **objects** – the tools the agents will use

- **causality** – the effects, both intended and unintended, of carrying out the actions

- **context** – the many details surrounding the agents and actions

- **surprises** – the unexpected things that happen in the story.

Klein proposes that a great deal can be learnt from the analysis of stories and that – whilst this is not scientific because the conditions cannot be controlled – it is possible for people hearing a story being told, to learn about motivation, intentions, pick up some ideas and fathom some of the mysteries.

Klein believes a story records an event that happened within a natural context, and in a way is a report of an experiment, linking cause and effect. It says 'under these conditions this is what happens'; and Klein suggests that we like stories because they are like reports of research projects, only easier to understand, remember and use.

He gives the example of jurors in a trial and how they make sense of the evidence. The decision-makers (jurors) try to assemble the facts into a story because the task of holding all the evidence in their heads without this is too difficult.

Klein suggests that story telling can help in making a diagnosis. In troubleshooting a piece of equipment, a technician can build a story of what might have gone wrong to explain a set of observed symptoms. Klein suggests that if troubleshooting and stories are viewed in the same way, we can apply the criteria of good stories to get a sense of how troubleshooting proceeds. The trouble-shooter is trying to detect a causal chain that leads from the initial conditions to the fault. By developing different explanations of what might be happening and then using this to gather more information the technician is undertaking a method of problem solving, both using the current state of knowledge and modifying it or building on it to move forward to diagnosis.

Klein suggests that stories are the most powerful method he has found for eliciting knowledge.

He suggests that if you ask experts to tell you what makes them so good at their job they will give general, non-specific answers but if you get them to tell you about tough cases – non-routine events where their skill made the difference – you will have a pathway into their perspective. Klein calls this method of eliciting information **The Critical Decision Method**, because it focuses attention on the key judgements and decisions that were made during an incident being described.

95

Klein uses an example of a piece of work undertaken by his team that involved one of his evaluators talking to a group of neonatal nurses and asking them how they spotted the early signs of sepsis (septic infection). They told her it was a mixture of intuition and experience. It was only when the evaluator listened to all the stories that experienced nurses told of what exactly they observed, that she could draw up a master list of clues to sepsis.

This toolkit will relate Klein's Critical decision method to the assessment of children and families in social work. The approach of story telling forms the basis of a framework for helping practitioners to reflect on the decisions made during the progress of a child's case through the system. This framework is designed to help practitioners in their analysis, understanding and consequently in their explanation of what influenced the various decisions. The method is not so much seen as a way of developing checklists that can be applied in other situations, as an attempt to build knowledge and understanding that could aid personal and professional development and be articulated within a team or across agencies and in reports.

The method that Klein uses with his team is to first of all find a good story; one with lots of expertise, perceptual skills and judgements. These aren't necessarily the dramatic stories, because often in those extremely dramatic situations there hasn't been the need to make subtle judgements and difficult decisions, as they tend to lead to rapid intuitive decisions. The stories they preferred were non-routine, complex stories where a novice might have faltered. The team developed a strategy for conducting interviews with practitioners and eliciting the information in a consistent way that allowed for the maximum reflection.

The method described by Klein is to make four passes through a story.

Pass 1   Ask for brief telling of the story to see if it has good possibilities and to identify the important parts so as not to waste time on trivialities.

Pass 2   A full telling of the story, pinning the details down to a timeline to get a better sense of what happened and to visualise (in a diagram) when things occured and how long they took. If possible, the diagram identifies where one stage of knowledge transformed into another.

Pass 3   Revisit the story and probe the thought processes. Ask the person to answer the following questions.

- At what points did you change your assessment of the situation?
- What alternative goals may have existed at certain points?
- What other courses of action were available to the ones taken?
- What factors might have led to the chosen option?
- Ask hypothetical questions, such as what might have happened here if a particular piece of information had not arrived or if another agent in the story had acted in a different way?
- If a particular option had been blocked, what would their reaction have been?
- What would they have done or thought if something that happened hadn't happened?
- What might their assumptions have been?

Pass 4   Klein suggests that at each choice or decision point, you ask: Would a novice get confused? What mistakes could they make? Why would they make them?

Further to Klein's suggestions, ask the questions: what would be the possible consequences of a different decision; or if certain factors came into play at the different decision points? Then reflect on what has been learnt from completing the timeline.

In Klein's team they take a long time to learn how to undertake these interviews and gather the right information, probe the right areas and spot when expertise comes into play. For this toolkit, however, the technique needed to be developed into an exercise that could be:

■ undertaken by an individual practitioner to aid their own reflection

■ used by a team manager in supervision to help a practitioner reflect on a case

■ undertaken as a peer-development exercise in pairs

■ facilitated in a team-development session, either by an external facilitator or a team member, to aid team learning.

As part of the Putting analysis into assessment project, individual practitioners ran through the exercise a number of times; and several practitioners ran through their stories with team colleagues present. Practitioners commented that unpicking the stories in this way helped them to understand how their own values and assumptions often influenced the decisions they made; and it also helped them to recognise when they were drawing on experience, theory or research findings to inform their own decision-making.

One practitioner was particularly struck by how strongly his many years' experience of working with a substance-misusing parent led to a set of unconscious assumptions, which directed many of his actions.

Another practitioner was alarmed to realise that, despite a mentally ill mother she was working with being from a very different cultural background, she has almost overlooked this in the context of looking at the impact of the mental health issues on the mother–child relationship.

In one session with a whole team, a practitioner demonstrated how her own refusal to be drawn into the hysteria within and around a particular family enabled the child's need to remain central to decision-making.

The practice tool presented here is a template for logging the decision points on a timeline and contains a number of trigger questions to ask to promote reflection.

Critical decision tool

Stage 1 Write a very brief, broad, brush-stroke outline of the overall situation, no more than two or three lines. Consider whether this is a promising story for using in the exercise. Does it have examples of expertise, perceptual skills and judgements?

Stage 3 At each of the decision points ask some or all of the following questions.

- What factors influenced the decision? (e.g. research theory, resources, pragmatic considerations)

- Note points when you changed your understanding of the situation and say why.

- Note when a decision changed the direction of the story. How did this impact on your thinking and actions?

- What alternative goals may have existed at certain points?

- What courses of action were available other than the ones taken?

- What factors may have led to the chosen option?

- What might have happened at certain points if a particular piece of information had not arrived or if another agent in the story had acted in a different way?

- If a particular option had been blocked, what would your reaction have been?

Stage 2 Log decision points on the line; and note on this side what they were and when they were made. Include decisions made by other agents in the story as well as those made by you. Also include micro-decisions that may have impacted on the overall progress of the story

Stage 4
Revisit the decision points and ask if a novice could have got confused and made mistakes? Why would they have made them? Consider what the possible consequences of different decision and/or factors coming into play would be at the different decision points? Reflect on what the learning has been from completing the timeline.

CASE STUDY 4.2

Critical decision tool

Background information

Single mother with four children (two grown-up ones) with three different fathers, none of whom live with or have much contact with the family.

Maureen – mother (White Irish)

Paul – 17-year-old son (Mixed parentage – Irish/Black Caribbean)

Rosa – 11-year-old daughter (Mixed parentage – Irish/Indian)

Sarah-Jane – 9-year-old daughter (Mixed parentage – Irish/Indian)

Jason – 8-year-old son (Mixed parentage – Irish/Indian)

Sam – 5-year-old son (White/Irish). Exhibiting behaviour problems in school although is popular. CAMHS assessment – mild learning difficulty. Learning difficulty and behaviour holding him back.

Mum has a history of using social services to get financial help.

School concerned.

Maureen takes good care of the children generally/some mild depression.

Child psychologist had expressed concerns re. Sam being aggressive in the home.

Referral from school – Sam has a bruise on face allegedly caused by his brother Paul having hit him.

What factors influenced decisions?	Log decision points on the line; and note on this side what they were.
	Unallocated.
Previous knowledge of team	
Previously decided was 'child in need' (CIN). (Team and agency culture influence here.) Needed worker – good case for worker (Derek) to gain experience.	Allocated new social worker, Derek, for assessment of need.
Was first case for Derek and he wanted to explain to Maureen that there was a need to protect Sam but why it was not a Section 47 response. Also to observe.	Undertook joint visit with Linda (supervisor) (announced).
Maureen and Sam open to/willing for assessment. Influenced by Paul's age – adult. Treated as vulnerable young person.	Decision to see Sam and work directly with him.
Didn't need to challenge mum.	2nd visit – saw Paul and Sam separately and together.
'That's what we do' – bring everyone together to share knowledge, establish partnership working. Got school's perspective and get pupil referral unit and school talking – common aims. Increased school's understanding of Sam's home situation.	Thorough assessment of their home environment and knowledge about children's needs.
To prevent breakdown between mum and school. Belief in behaviourist approach.	Decision to hold network meeting. Mum invited.
Behaviour management. Anger, frustration about his father. Aim to help him recognise where anger comes from.	Decision for mum and school to communicate and use prizes and rewards to try and improve Sam's behaviour.
Thresholds/eligibility/politics/gate-keeping/Paul open about problems to Derek and willing to have counselling and thought he might work with them.	Refer Paul to counselling (will be a family consultation).
Wanted to encourage mum's independence (history of using services/getting to crisis). Low motivation due to depression and mum defining other priorities (e.g. losing weight).	(Adolescents team would not take because not mental health, so family approach required – Child and Family Consultation Service did take referral.)
Mum being quite positive.	Plans to refer mum to parent support group. Was a plan to refer mum to voluntary family support service for family work but mum not keen and not happening yet.
Importance of having an outlet. Build self-esteem. Positive effects on relationships at home. Divert from potential anti-social activities.	Decision to try and get all kids involved in more activities. 'Positive activities' programme.
Paul feeling a scapegoat. To build on network meeting, previous assessments, shift mum's description of Paul's problems.	Decision to encourage view of Paul as a role model. To try and encourage mum to use positive reinforcement, consistency.

Putting Analysis into Assessment

[additional information]

First home visit met Mum and kids. Second visit met Paul.

Undertook core assessment.

Wanted to try and promote Mum's independence from SSD.

Decision to work with Sam and Paul directly because of nature of referral.

Network meeting – gave overall picture, discussed schooling and pupil referral unit.

House very tidy.

Children polite and well behaved. Paul friendly, polite, always there, articulate, agreed to go to counselling.

Relied on Mum's account. Sam gets in moods and Paul gets irritated.

Mum finds it difficult to get outside. House dark, curtains drawn, kids cooped up watching TV. four-bed flat.

Need opportunities after school and to get out.

Bruise was on head.

Bullying behaviour?

Mum open about it happening, cried at network meeting.

Paul upfront.

Referral made for Paul to go to counselling.

Anger towards his dad. Appreciated male figure (Derek) taking interest.

Sam took it hardest when his dad left (2 years ago).

Paul's dad not been around for years.

Mum previously distanced from children, gets very low and lacks self-esteem, comfort eats. Less likely to go out. On benefits.

School – put in various steps/measures.

Consistency between school & home in managing behaviour.

Educational psychologist recommended SEN statement.

Could a novice have made mistakes or different decisions? What would have happened?

- Worker was fairly inexperienced but well supervised. Without supervision, may have not seen whole picture.

- Worker was wondering at times what they were doing – sometimes difficult to see the wood for the trees.

- Agency team culture had a large part to play in route taken, i.e. keeping cases in CIN rather than in Section 47 if appropriate and possible.

- Family were open to intervention – different decision may have had to be taken if not.

- Saw the two children, Paul and Sam, separately as well as working with whole family – if hadn't taken this approach one part of system could have benefited without improvement in another, risk of problem reoccurring.

- The assessment of needs led to the identification of appropriate services. If needs not met, difficulties could have been compounded.

- Partnership approach – improvements in family relationships were noted and built on – if this approach not taken, family may have become demotivated.

- Ongoing support was available rather than pressure to close case – which may have led to problem reoccurring.

- Working on building networks of support to prevent isolation in future.

Critical decision tool

Aim

To introduce Klein's ideas about story telling as a method for reflecting on and understanding decisions; and to test out the critical decision method in practice.

Methods

- In advance of the session, select two participants to use the Critical decision tool to talk through one of their cases. Ask them to choose, preferably, a case where an assessment is complete and which illustrates the complexity of decision-making. Ask them to write a brief summary paragraph, with basic factual information only, in advance of the session and to have copies to hand out at the session.

- Begin the session by asking participants if they feel they currently have time and opportunity to revisit case decision-making and to reflect, either alone or with colleagues, on how and why certain decisions have been made and what might have happened if these decisions had been different. If people feel they do have these opportunities then ask them to describe how, when what, with whom and so forth.

- Introduce Klein's work to the group with a brief presentation using the notes above (under 'Critical decision method').

- Distribute the blank critical decision timeline (page 98) and explain that this has been developed from Klein's ideas during the Putting analysis into assessment project.

- Suggest ways in which it might be used – for example, in a session such as this, for personal reflection, in co-working, in supervision, and in preparing reports for court – to organise thinking.

- Tell the group how two participants were invited to each write a paragraph on their cases before the session. Tell the group who the participants are.

- Stress to the group that the participants are very brave and thank them in advance for exposing their practice. Remind everyone to be positive and supportive in their questions.

- Have some prompt cards prepared, each with one of the following points written on it:
  - Research
  - Theory
  - Evidence of involvement of child
  - Evidence of partnership with parents
  - Interagency working
  - Hypothesising
  - Cultural review
  - Focus on needs
  - Checklists/resources

- Give out the cards so that each participant holds one.

■ Ask the first presenting participant to introduce their case and hand out the summary.

■ Make four passes through the case by doing the following.

- Invite the participant to present a very brief summary.

- Ask the participant to go though the case in more detail, identifying the decision points. Meanwhile, draw a timeline on the flip chart and add the decision points to it.

- Revisit key decision points and ask the participant questions about their decisions and those of others, based on the trigger points on the critical decision sheet. Focus on trying to tease out as much as possible about influences, motivations, constraints, and unexpected developments. Invite other participants to ask questions, using their prompt card to focus their questions.

- Go through the case one more time, asking whether less- or more-experienced practitioners might have behaved differently. Ask what effect this might have had.

■ Encourage general discussion. If necessary, prompt the group with questions such as: Has the exercise raised particular issues? (Be sure to check that the presenting participants feel comfortable and not too exposed.) What does the practitioner learn from this exercise? What do others in the team learn? Do you feel that this would be a useful exercise to do when you are reporting on your assessments or preparing court reports? Would it be beneficial for you to do this on a regular basis with the team? Does it indicate to you a need for further training and development or other actions?

5. Team development activities

This chapter contains a range of resources for use by team managers or external facilitators during team meetings, on team away days or in practice development sessions, to assist in the development of a culture of reflection and analysis within the team. Apart from the peer review exercise these activities are not case specific; and are designed to open up discussion about analysis.

Activity 1

What is analysis?

Aim

To develop a shared understanding of what is understood by analysis.

Objectives

By the end of the activity participants will have:

- expressed thoughts and ideas about analysis and how and when it takes place, who should be involved and how it relates to other elements of assessment

- discussed a common understanding of the meaning of analysis

- gained a common understanding of the definition of analysis and how it relates to judgement and decision-making.

Time

30–45 minutes.

Ideal numbers

Teams of between four and 12 (up to 20 if on a training course).

Method

- Invite the participants to form pairs.

- Distribute the What is analysis? handout (page 107), one to each pair.

- Ask the participants, in their pairs, to discuss and answer the questions. Tell them they will have 15 minutes for this.

- When the 15 minutes are up, reconvene the full group.

- Ask for feedback from the group, taking each question in turn.

- Encourage a group discussion in which analysis' main components and facets are agreed.

Facilitator's notes

This exercise is a useful starting point for undertaking some exploration about the quality of analysis within a team, as it provides an opportunity to reflect together on what we mean by analysis. What you will tend to find is that analysis, in the participants' view, is made up of several components, which get drawn out and made explicit through the exercise. Also you will find that on training courses analysis means pretty much the same thing to most people, but there is a huge number of ways of describing it and different emphases on what is involved.

There is no 'right' answer to this exercise, although there could potentially be some wrong ones! Give out the following dictionary definition as a guide to the way participants should be thinking about analysis.

> The division of a physical or abstract whole into its constituent parts to examine or determine their relationship ... a statement of the results of this.
>
> *Collins Concise Dictionary*

And offer the following example of a wrong answer: 'information gathering' is not analysis nor is 'data management' but these are essential components.

What is analysis?

■ What do you understand the word analysis to mean?

■ What part does analysis play in assessments of need?

■ How do you go about analysis – what does it involve?

■ At what stage of an assessment do you analyse?

■ Who might be involved in the analysis and how?

■ How is analysis distinct from planning and decision-making?

■ How does it relate to them?

Activity 2

SWOT analysis of the team's strengths and weaknesses

Aim

To provide a health check of analytical practice in the team and to develop action planning to address issues arising.

Objectives

By the end of the activity participants will have:

- reflected on the strengths, weaknesses, opportunities, and threats relating to their own personal practice

- reflected on the strengths, weaknesses, opportunities, and threats relating to the practice across the team as a whole

- had an opportunity to address any gaps and deficits

- articulated and recorded examples of the team's strengths and weaknesses in analysis

- identified actions to strengthen practice.

Time

1½–2 hours.

Ideal numbers

Any number, but if doing the activity with more than one team and breaking into groups, a total of no more than 24 people.

Method

- Draw a SWOT box, as shown below, on a flip chart or whiteboard.

Strengths	Weaknesses
Opportunities	Threats

- Using the following explanation, go through the SWOT analysis model and method. Explain that the method for completing the SWOT is to agree the following.

- **The strengths** – these are examples of how analytical practice is tangibly strong and positive, e.g. 'assessment reports commended by senior managers'.

- **Weaknesses** – where there are tangible deficits and weaknesses in practice, lack of confidence, competence, knowledge and skills, e.g. 'lack of use of evidence in reports'.

- **Opportunities** – what exists within the team, agency and wider environment, which will support the development of more analytical practice, e.g. 'PQ programme'.

- **Threats** – what factors create obstacles to the development of more analytical practice in the team, e.g. 'volume of work', 'timescales'.

■ Take each of the SWOT boxes in the order they appear above, asking the team members to shout out examples to place for each one. Record all suggestions in the box you are dealing with, unless they definitely fit into another category in which case they should be written down there. Continue until all the SWOT boxes are completed.

■ Tackle the next exercise either as the whole group or invite participants to form smaller groups. Revisit each area of the SWOT box and ask what needs to happen in the team (or agency) to support the strong areas and address the deficits. Record the participants' responses as a list of points.

■ Explain that the next task is to make the list of points practicable by identifying who will need to carry out each action; and by adding a timescale for when it should be completed. Ideally, any tasks arising from this exercise should be spread out amongst the team and not all ascribed to the team manager.

■ Encourage groups to log actions that they feel should be taken – even if they feel they are outside their scope. Encourage discussion and seek agreement about how these points can be fed into the wider organisation or even beyond, for example through a team manager or external networks.

■ The template below is useful for recording action planning.

Action	By whom	By when	Support/resources required	Outcome

Facilitator's notes

If the facilitator is the team manager, this exercise needs to be handled sensitively, allowing the team to come up with their own examples of strengths and weaknesses; whilst taking opportunities where appropriate to praise good practice and highlight weaknesses if the team don't come up with these themselves.

There is also a possibility that team members will wish to highlight deficits in management and supervision. One way to make this less personal is to divide the group into two or three smaller groups and give them a blank SWOT sheet to complete themselves and then put all the completed sheets on the wall. This will allow for acknowledgement of issues raised without it being too uncomfortable.

Activity 3

Scaling exercise

Aim

To ascertain how participants perceive their ability individually and as a team to undertake a thorough and balanced analysis.

Objectives

By the end of the activity participants will have:

■ identified what helps and what hinders thinking analytically throughout an assessment; and how much the culture of their agency supports analysis

■ discussed the use of a scaling system for demonstrating their responses to a number of questions about analysis

■ gained a clearer picture of the perspectives and experiences of colleagues in relation to analysis as part of the assessment process.

Time

45 minutes to an hour.

Ideal numbers

4–16.

Method

■ Make up ten separate cards with bold, clear numbers on (1–10), and lay them out in numerical order in a line on the floor, leaving sufficient space between them for a number of people to stand on one without spilling over onto the next.

■ Tell participants that you will be reading out a series of statements and will want them to stand on the number that most accurately reflects their response, with 1 being completely **disagree** and 10 being completely **agree.**

■ Read the first of the statements (see box).

- The assessment framework helps practitioners to analyse information more systematically.

- The culture in my team (or agency) supports reflective analytical practice.

- I feel confident and competent in my knowledge of research and theory and in my ability to apply this to practice.

- There are some areas of practice where I find it harder to use my analytical skills than others.

- Developing a more analytical approach is pointless because you have to fit children's and families' needs into existing services in the end anyway.

- Supervision helps me to develop a more analytical approach and be reflective.

- I have a range of tools at my disposal to help in gathering information.

- I have a range of tools at my disposal to help in analysing information.

■ Ask participants to place themselves along the scale of 0–10, according to the extent to which they agree or disagree with the statement just read out.

■ Ask those participants standing at the extreme ends of the scale why they have placed themselves there. Ideally, ask a couple of participants at each end and then ask those next to them until you reach the centre.

■ Invite a couple of participants towards the bottom end of the scale (nearest '0') what would need to happen to enable them to move further up the scale. Ask people who are a little further towards the top end (nearer '10') as well.

■ Allow around five to ten minutes altogether for discussion of the statement.

■ Read the second statement in the box.

■ Repeat the process (from 'Ask participants to place') until each statement in the box has been read out and acted upon.

■ Round off the session by summarising what has been learnt from the exercise and highlighting interesting points.

Facilitator's notes

If there is fruitful discussion that carries on for longer over one point, you can reduce the number of statements. Take care not to let any one discussion go on for longer than ten minutes as the group's concentration will lapse (and they will get tired of standing up).

Depending on your reasons for undertaking this exercise, you may want to capture some of what is said, in which case it is a good idea to choose a scribe to make a note, as this exercise can lead to some interesting points being made by participants as to why they have placed themselves on a particular number.

Where there are obvious trends, with most people standing in roughly the same place, this provides useful information; as do the views of those who stand alone.

This exercise has always, without fail, led to a rich discussion – with a variety of views being expressed and points debated.

Activity 4

Assessing the culture of analysis within a team

Aim

To obtain detailed knowledge about individual practitioner's analytical skills; to what extent they are confident in the tools and resources available to them, and their knowledge of research and theory.

Objectives

By the end of the activity participants will have:

■ given detailed feedback on a number of questions relevant to their own analytical skills and their perception of what happens within their team (this will provide useful team information and an opportunity for reflection and planning)

■ created a detailed record of the team's perspective on factors that contribute to a sound analysis of the information gathered during an assessment.

Time

This exercise needs to be done over a period of a week or two. Completing the questionnaire should take no more than half an hour; analysing the results, two hours; giving feedback to the team with discussion, one to one-and-a-half hours.

Ideal numbers

Everyone in the team/organisation.

Method

■ Arrange for distribution and completion of the Questionnaire for practitioners (page 113) in advance of the session: in a development or team session, within a team meeting or in a practice development meeting.

■ Also in advance of the session, collate the responses or arrange for the teams to collate them. To collate the findings from the questionnaire, count up the responses and record them and any comments on one copy of the form. It is likely that some themes will emerge, such as common views on the culture, difficult cases and the like. This collated information should help in planning a learning/development programme for the team in future.

■ Once the analysis of the questionnaire is complete, give feedback to the team on the trends and learning requirements that arose from it. Record any issues of concern so that they can be taken forward and a plan drawn up to address them. This record can be viewed alongside the SWOT analysis (page 108) and used as a planning tool.

Facilitator's notes

It is important to ensure that you have time to analyse the responses. As it will take at least two hours, do not start the process if you are unable to complete it.

Questionnaire for practitioners: Putting analysis into assessment project

Purpose of questionnaire: To find out and explore what influences a practitioner's ability to analyse and exercise professional judgement in their decision-making during the assessment process.

1. Name (optional).. Length of time in team.. How long qualified	
2. Do you think your assessments are needs led? Please specify what you have found as barriers to carrying out needs-led assessment.	(Please circle the answer you agree with) Never / Sometimes / Always
3. Do you use the departmental or DH (2000) format in recording your assessments?	Yes / No
4. (Please circle the appropriate response in the right-hand column) The form enables you to make an holistic assessment of a child's needs. The form leads you towards undertaking an analysis of the information gathered. I usually make explicit reference to any theories I have drawn on when recording my assessment. Comments (optional)...	Agree / Disagree / Neither Agree / Disagree / Neither Agree / Disagree / Neither
5. Are there some types of cases that you find particularly challenging when it comes to analysis and decision-making? (please circle your response in the right-hand column) If 'yes', please give details (please tick categories that you find personally challenging) Sexual abuse ☐ Children beyond parental control ☐ Physical abuse ☐ Pre-birth assessments ☐ Neglect ☐ Disabled children ☐ Parental mental health ☐ Family conflict or breakdown ☐ Parental substance misuse ☐ Domestic violence ☐ Other ☐ please give details:...	Yes / No

Putting Analysis into Assessment

6. I always feel well supported in the decision-making process.

    My decisions are challenged in a supportive way.

    Supervision provides the opportunity to reflect on my analysis of a case.

    There is time and space in team meetings to reflect on and discuss decisions made in assessments.

    There are opportunities for informal discussion with peers to assist in analysis and decision-making.

Agree / Disagree / Neither	
Agree / Disagree / Neither	
Agree / Disagree / Neither	
Agree / Disagree / Neither	
Agree / Disagree / Neither	

7. Generally, analysis and decision-making in my practice are influenced by the following factors (please try and allocate percentages next to each one, i.e. to add up to 100%)

    (Mark as percentages totalling 100%)

    Formal knowledge   ....

    Reasoning skills   ....

    Values   ....

    Practice wisdom   ....

    Emotional wisdom   ....

    Comments   ....

    ....

    ....

    ....

    ....

8. Please indicate (by circling the appropriate responses in the box opposite) which of the following sources of formal knowledge you draw on to assist you in analysis and decision-making.

    Theory relating to specific issues in child welfare (e.g. attachment theory/ child development/ecological theory)

    A lot/Sometimes/Occasionally Not at all

    Research about child welfare and social care

    A lot/Sometimes/Occasionally Not at all

    Theory relating to areas other than children's social care

    A lot/Sometimes/Occasionally Not at all

    Government policy and guidance

    A lot/Sometimes/Occasionally Not at all

    Please indicate three pieces of research or theory, which have significantly informed your professional judgement in analysis and decision-making.

    ....

    ....

    ....

9. (Please tick any of the statements you agree with)
    Regularly seek expert opinion from external professionals/specialists to inform my analysis and decision-making. ☐

    ....

    I normally involve all professionals, who are involved with the family or child, in the assessment process. ☐

    ....

    Most professionals involved in the family willingly take an active role in the assessment process. ☐

    ....

    There are some professionals who are difficult to engage in assessments. ☐
    (If box on right ticked for the above question, please select and tick from list below)

    Schools ☐
    Youth service ☐
    Family aides ☐
    YOTS ☐
    GP ☐
    Connexions ☐
    CAMHS ☐
    HV ☐
    Foster carers ☐
    School nurse ☐
    Voluntary sector ☐
    Police ☐
    Family centres ☐
    Adult substance misuse ☐
    Adult mental health ☐
    Others ☐ (please give details)

    ....

    ....

    The assessment format encourages meaningful input from other professionals. ☐

    Comments ....

    ....

    ....

10. (Please circle the response closest to your own in the box opposite)
    I involve children in assessment in the following ways, by:

    Seeking children's views with parent/carer present — Always / Often / Sometimes / Never

    Seeking children's views confidentially — Always / Often / Sometimes / Never

    Using specific tools for communicating with children or undertaking direct work sessions — Always / Often / Sometimes / Never

    Showing children the completed assessment (or explaining it to them) — Always / Often / Sometimes / Never

    Getting children and young people to sign off the assessment — Always / Often / Sometimes / Never

    Involving children directly in CP conferences and reviews — Always / Often / Sometimes / Never

    Involving children directly in LAC reviews — Always / Often / Sometimes / Never

    Informing children of their rights and of the Children's rights service — Always / Often / Sometimes / Never

Putting Analysis into Assessment

11. [Please circle appropriate response in the right-hand column) I involve parents/carers in the assessment in the following ways, by:	
Interviewing parents/carers in the office	Always / Often / Sometimes / Never
Interviewing parents/carers in their home	Always / Often / Sometimes / Never
Observing parent/carer–child interaction	Always / Often / Sometimes / Never
Asking parents/carers to complete self-assessment scales or exercises (DH or others)	Always / Often / Sometimes / Never
Routinely asking parents/carers to read the completed assessment and recording their agreement (or otherwise).	Always / Often / Sometimes / Never
Having parents/carers routinely sign assessments, etc.	Always / Often / Sometimes / Never
Comments	
12. Please tick the opportunities for learning that you have engaged in over the last 6 months.	
Team-based discussion development session	☐
Local training for social workers	☐
Local inter-agency training	☐
Training or conferences out of the local area	☐
'Research in practice', 'Making research count' seminars or briefings, or similar.	☐
13. Do you generally feel that there are sufficient opportunities, through training and development, for accessing knowledge that would assist you in analysing decision-making and exercising professional judgement? If 'no', please indicate below what you would like to access but are currently unable to.	Yes / No

Putting Analysis into Assessment

Activity 5

Peer review of assessments

Aim

To encourage peer mentoring and practice sharing in the team in relation to analysis.

Objectives

By the end of the activity participants will have:

■ given constructive feedback to each other about the quality of analysis in assessments

■ shared experience and expertise across the team

■ reflected on peer review of assessments.

Time

1½ hours, plus preparation of 3–4 hours.

Ideal numbers

6–12 (need an even number).

Method

■ In advance of the session, ask each practitioner to identify and provide you with an assessment they have completed that is fairly typical of their practice. To make the selection more random, suggest that each practitioner uses his or her last assessment.

■ Use a code to mark which assessment belongs to which participant as this will prove useful later on.

■ Attach a feedback sheet (page 118) to the back of each assessment.

■ Also in advance of the session, read each assessment and make a note of its strengths and weaknesses, particularly in relation to analysis, using the trigger questions on the feedback sheet.

■ Invite participants to form pairs.

■ Distribute two assessments to each pair, using the codes to make sure that no one is looking at their own.

■ Invite participants to read through each assessment and note the strengths and areas for improvement on the attached feedback sheet, using the trigger questions as prompts. Tell the pairs of participants that they will have at least 20–30 minutes to discuss and comment on each assessment.

■ After 20–30 minutes, collect the assessments and then use the codes to help you redistribute them to their authors.

■ Tell participants that they now have 15 minutes to read the comments written on their assessment.

■ After 15 minutes, encourage the participants, still in their pairs, to discuss their response to the comments.

■ Reconvene the group and invite feedback from everyone, as individuals. Prompt with questions such as: Was it helpful to have this feedback? Did it ring true or were you surprised by the comments? Is there anything you would like to ask, for clarification? How has it left you feeling? Are there any actions you will take as a result?

Facilitator's notes

It is important that all assessments provided are of the same type, that is they should all be initial or all core assessments. This exercise can work for both types but core assessments will take more time. Using core assessments may provide opportunities for a more in-depth examination and reflection.

In some teams it would be possible to encourage direct discussion between those writing the comments and those in receipt. The notes that you, as facilitator, made (concerning strengths and areas for improvement) can also be offered as part of the discussion. There is a risk of participants feeling exposed or becoming defensive. Judgement will need to be used to decide how far to take the discussion and whether it is likely to be helpful and productive for the individual participants and the team as a whole.

Feedback sheet

Trigger questions

Is the assessment needs-led?

Have parents and children and other professionals been appropriately involved?

Is there evidence of differing hypotheses being considered and tested out?

Is there evidence of any analysis of the facts or weighing up of options?

Is there any evidence of research or theory being used to support arguments?

Do actions flow logically from the information gathered and its analysis?

Have decisions been discussed with children and carers?

Strengths	Areas for improvement

Activity 6

Miracle question exercise

Aim

To encourage team members to be imaginative in describing their aspirations for children and for practice in their team.

Objectives

By the end of the activity participants will have:

■ drawn from solution-focused work and 'thought outside the box' to imagine what practice in the team could be like

■ created a series of tangible aspirational statements about the way in which practice could develop in the team and agency

■ created an action plan to work towards these aspirational statements.

Time

From 1–3 hours depending on how far the exercise is taken.

Ideal numbers

Any number.

Method

■ Ask participants to close their eyes and relax. Explain that they are going to be taken on a guided fantasy.

■ Read out the following paragraph slowly, pausing to allow people time to think at the relevant points.

Imagine that when you go to sleep tonight, a miracle occurs and three years pass. During that time, everything has changed and assessment practice has improved in your team and agency; so now analysis is an integral part of assessments; decisions and actions flowing from assessment are needs led, completely appropriate and most likely to lead to the best outcomes for children and their families; and there are opportunities for reflection and team learning.

■ Tell participants that they will be asked a number of questions; and that they will be given about 30 seconds to answer each. Stress that they will not be sharing their answers yet.

■ Ask the following questions, allowing 30 seconds between each one for participants to think about their responses.
  - When you wake up and go into work what will you immediately notice has changed?
  - How will you personally be behaving?
  - How will practitioners and managers be behaving?
  - How will the atmosphere in the team have changed?
  - How will children and parents be behaving?
  - Will there be other visual evidence of changes?
  - How will other professionals be behaving?

120

■ If participants have closed their eyes, ask them to open them now.

■ Repeat the first question and invite participants to shout out the thoughts they had in response to it. Record all responses on a flip chart – even if they are light-hearted.

■ Do the same for each of the subsequent questions (that is, repeat the question and record the shouted out answers).

■ Examine the lists that have been made and ask participants to reflect on how far the current situation in their workplace is from the idealised picture.

■ Ask the team to try and prioritise three or four areas in which they could work towards achieving change. **Note:** If it is a large team, divide it up into two or three smaller groups, then ask each group to identify three priority areas each; and then reconvene the whole group to debate and agree the top three to five priorities.

■ Once the priorities are agreed, ask the team to develop an action plan to achieve these; for example, by answering key questions concerning what/when/who uses the action planning template (page 109). Stress the importance of ascribing tasks to named people and agreeing a timescale. Record the action plan and agree a date on which to review progress.

Facilitator's notes

This exercise does require that participants leave behind their everyday constraints and be imaginative, so some judgement will have to be exercised as to how ready a team or group are to do this. If they are feeling stressed or bogged down, this type of activity might feel a bit too esoteric. On the other hand, it could be a welcome relief. There is room for some humour here and people will make some 'off the wall' suggestions but try to take everything on board and facilitate the team in prioritising actions that are likely to bear some fruit and be most useful to the team's development.

6. Training course programmes

Below are some sample training programmes that show how to combine the activities in the book to create a training course programme. There are supporting PowerPoint presentations, for use with these programmes.

The suggested formats include a two-day programme, which is ideal for exploring the concepts in depth and a one-day programme, if time is limited. The two-day programme can be broken down (breaking at lunch) into four half-day sessions run over a period of time, if necessary.

During the Putting analysis into assessment project, a series of half-day programmes like these were used several times, usually with anything from a week to a month between sessions. It is a good idea, in this case, to encourage participants to do some reading between sessions and, if possible, to try out the material that has been introduced. If participants do this, then build in some time at the start of each session for them to give feedback on their experience of using the materials in practice.

Sessions of this type can also be run for first-line managers or practice managers. Here it is important to stress the usefulness of the materials to supervision, case planning and practice development in their teams.

These programmes have all been tested in practice and have received positive feedback.

Although timings have been ascribed to all activities, there is room for some flexibility, depending on group size and the actual time available. More time was allowed for activities taking place within discrete practice development sessions than for those within training courses.

PUTTING ANALYSIS INTO ASSESSMENT

Two-day training course programme

Aims

To increase practitioner skills and confidence in analysis and judgement-making within assessment practice with children in need.

Objectives

■ To explore the policy and practice context of making decisions and judgements.

■ To provide an opportunity to assess strengths and weaknesses in use of analysis in assessment.

■ To introduce models and approaches that will strengthen assessment practice with children in need.

Day one

10.00	Aims, objectives and ground rules
10.15	Warm-up and introductions
10.30	Introduction

Presentation 7: Putting analysis into assessment. Use some or all of the slides from this presentation to inform participants about the Putting Analysis into Assessment Project and to set the context for the course.

10.50	Activity 1: What is Analysis?
11.30	*Break*
11.45	Activity 3: Scaling exercise
12.15	Analysis or intuition?

Presentation 1: Analysis, intuition and the nature of expertise and Practice development session 1: The nature of expertise, sections c), d), e), g) or i), and h).

1.00	*Lunch*
1.45	Back to basics: Needs assessment

Practice development session 4: Needs analysis – introduction and stage 1.

2.15	Using social research methods

Presentation 2: Analysing, hypothesising and reporting, up to slide 6.

2.25	Practice development session 2: Cultural review – sections b to e
3.15	*Break*
3.30	Practice development session 3: Hypothesising – sections d to g
4.20–4.30	Discussion and *close*

Day two

10.00	Warm-up and reflection on Day One
10.15	Practice development session 5: The signs of safety approach – section a, then either run through b – f, or g and h.
	In both cases invite discussion and feedback at the end.
11.30	*Break*
11.45	Practice development session 6: Involving children – either Exercise 1 and Presentation 5, inviting discussion on the issues involved, or Exercise 2, Presentation 5 and Option 1.
12.45	*Lunch*
1.30	Practice development session 7: Decision tree
	You may also want to use some of the later slides from presentation 1
3.00	*Break*
3.15	Practice development session 9: Conclusions and reporting – either Activity 1 or Activity 2
4.15	Final evaluations and feedback
4.30	*Close*

PUTTING ANALYSIS INTO ASSESSMENT

One-day training course programme

Aims

To increase practitioner skills and confidence in analysis and judgement-making within assessment practice with children in need.

Objectives

■ To explore the policy and practice context of making decisions and judgements.

■ To provide an opportunity to assess strengths and weaknesses in use of analysis in assessment.

■ To introduce models and approaches that will strengthen assessment practice with children in need.

Programme

Day one

10.00	Aims, objectives and ground rules
10.15	Introduction.
	Presentation 7: Putting analysis into assessment. Use some or all of the slides from this presentation to inform participants about the Putting Analysis into Assessment Project and to set the context for the course'
10.30	Activity 1: What is Analysis?'
11.00	*Break*
11.15	Analysis or intuition?
	Presentation 1: Analysis, intuition and the nature of expertise and Practice development session 1: The nature of expertise, sections c, d and e.
11.35	Practice development session 1: The nature of expertise, section g or sections i and h.
12.15	Back to basics: Needs assessment
	Practice development session 4: Needs analysis – introduction and stage 1
12.45	*Lunch*
1.45	Using social research methods
	Presentation 2: Analysing, hypothesising and reporting, up to slide 7
2.00	Practice development session 2: Cultural review, sections b to e.
	Practice development session 3: Hypothesising – sections d to g
3.00	*Break*
3.15	Practice development session 6: Involving children – either Exercise 1 and Presentation 5, inviting discussion on the issues involved, or Exercise 2, Presentation 5 and Option 1.
4.00	*Close*

7. Challenges and opportunities for analytical practice

This chapter discusses further some of the lessons to be drawn from the literature and the Putting analysis into assessment project regarding what helps and hinders analytical and reflective practice.

It goes on to consider the particular challenges that arise in multi-agency working and some of the things that can be done to reduce bias and distorted thinking.

It then makes suggestions as to what can be done at the team, supervisory and organisational level to create and sustain a practice culture that supports continuous learning and reflective practice. In particular, it considers how evidence-based practice can be promoted at every level within an organisation to turn the rhetoric into reality.

Lessons from the project

There were some general points made by participants during the Putting analysis into assessment project that it seems useful to consider here. The teams involved were drawn from two settings – which contrasted geographically, demographically and in terms of resources and challenges facing them – but the overall lessons learned from both areas were broadly similar. In both areas, feedback indicated that there were some important gains for the teams from being involved in the project which went some way to improving the analytical practice within the teams. These were: getting analysis firmly on their agenda; a heightened awareness of the pitfalls of using intuitive methods alone; and more focused attention on analytical approaches.

The introduction of theoretical notions about how to think critically and the passing on of the 'tools' included within this toolkit was, in the most part, received positively and has added to the practical resources available to team members. Significantly, the time and space that sessions allowed was as important as the use of the tools themselves. The practice development sessions where, instead of introducing tools and approaches, there was time to think about analysis (through case discussions, looking at each other's reports, examining conclusions and understanding decisions), were undoubtedly as useful to practitioners. It seemed that putting aside time for the practice development sessions in the presence of (or at least with the encouragement of) team managers, provided a much-needed opportunity for individual and team reflection. Furthermore, participants reported that once analysis was firmly on their team agendas there was more focus on it within supervision and in peer discussions.

The importance of reflection time as an essential prerequisite for undertaking good quality analysis within assessments arose time and again.

It is perhaps not surprising that resource issues, which impact on the time available to practitioners for reflection, pose one of the greatest challenges to analytical practice. In many agencies, limited resources lead to high volumes of work that, despite all intentions to the contrary, result in reactive practice. Additionally, many practitioners and some managers on the project highlighted that their ability to be needs-led in assessments was influenced significantly by an awareness of service constraints.

However, much can be done at an organisational level to enable practitioners to undertake assessments that thoroughly identify needs, both in order to help the agency meet them and to identify where they cannot do so. Some practitioners on the project told us of a tendency to see fixed timescales and deadlines for reports as dates by which they had to have finished assessments, even when they had established only a partial picture of the family's circumstances. This highlighted the importance of agencies supporting practitioners by encouraging them to acknowledge in reports 'how far they've got' in their assessments, in order that they do not feel under pressure to say more than they know.

The physical working environment also plays an important part, whilst open-plan offices can be conducive to receiving on-the-spot peer support they are also generally noisy. It is important that workers at all levels have opportunities to work in quiet rooms at times when they particularly need to focus on a specific piece of work or grapple with the meaning of lots of information to help them consider their analysis.

The ability of practitioners to draw critically on research findings and theory clearly plays an important part in efforts to improve analysis within the social work task. However, when we asked practitioners on the project and in training courses about their perceived levels of competence and confidence in drawing on research evidence and theory, they frequently responded that they did not have time available to them for reading, although nearly all of them wanted to be more aware of up-to-date research. Individual practitioners clearly had varying levels of confidence and competence; and levels of experience had an impact on this. Newly qualified practitioners often have up-to-date knowledge but need to build up their confidence in applying it in practice, whereas those who had been qualified for some time can think that their knowledge levels have lapsed. It is often the case with learning and experience that the more we learn the more we realise we need to learn. Another cause cited for low confidence levels was the frequent criticism of social workers through negative media portrayal and what some practitioners perceived as low expectations among professionals and families about their profession.

Social workers also often expressed the view that they were not seen as experts in the court arena and were reluctant to portray themselves as such. Some were reluctant to cite research evidence or to link their analysis to theory in their assessment reports because they did not think they had sufficient grasp of research to respond to the challenge they might meet in court. They expected that if other 'experts' were brought in to erode their arguments they might be 'setting themselves up' by using research and, in turn, all their reasoning would be called into question. This is an understandable concern and is compounded further if legal advisors and agencies are not clear with staff about what is expected of them with regard to using research evidence within reports. For this reason Research in Practice are undertaking a Change project called *Social work and the use of research evidence in relation to children's cases in the family court*, to examine and make recommendations in this difficult area.

Some of the factors that the project teams thought supported analytical practice were offered as follows.

- 'Supportive' team culture

- Constructive debate being encouraged within the team

- Good supervision [one team particularly noted the usefulness of having a manager who asks for their views before giving her own and who then challenges constructively]

- There was no such thing as a 'stupid question' [said one team]; and there is a 'safe atmosphere' for team members to learn and question things [said another]

- Joint work, particularly in complex and long-term cases, helps too; a second opinion from colleagues helps us [workers] keep sight of standards of care and 'thresholds' as family situations can become 'normalised' in the minds of workers through exposure to a family over time

- Drawing on theory and research findings

- Commitment by managers to professional development

- Ethnically and gender diverse teams reflective of local population

- Experienced team members

- Team study days

- External inter-agency forums.

It is clear that whilst social workers can do many things, including using tools such as those in this toolkit, to enhance their own practice, the systems they work within also need to support them in the task. What can be done at the organisational level to improve analytical practice is discussed below (under 'Creating and sustaining an environment for continuous practice development) but first, consideration needs to be given to the specific issues that arise in inter-agency working.

Reflection and analysis in multi-agency contexts

As discussed in the section on Preparing oneself in Chapter 2, page 11, any decisions that a practitioner makes is influenced by their emotions, values, reasoning skills, practice wisdom and formal knowledge. It is important (but not easy) for the practitioner to try and identify these influences in order to be transparent in their decisions, but even more so when there are a range of professionals involved with a decision. As well as each individual being encouraged to be reflective about their own personal and professional responses (as in reality these are rarely absolutely separable), they need to find ways to encourage agencies to bring an awareness of what norms and practices they bring to an assessment because of the context in which they work. Examples of such norms may be: thresholds, knowledge of resource availability and past experience of how their agency has worked in similar circumstances.

Whilst groups have the advantage of many heads instead of one, they also bring with them the potential for bias and distorted thinking – or 'Groupthink' as Janis (1982) called it – which are often caused by power issues and the avoidance of conflict. Munro (2002) summarised what Janis identified as the following tendencies when groups think together: an overestimation of the group; closed mindedness; and pressure to conform. Munro also summarised the following suggested measures designed to help to protect against groupthink.

1. Group leaders should explicitly encourage dissent and criticism including of their own position.

2. Group leaders should let the lowest ranking members of the group speak first and should themselves refrain from stating their personal preferences at the outset.

3. Groups should set up other groups with other leaders to consider the same question, allowing for a comparison of responses.

4. Group members should periodically discuss the group's deliberations with trusted associates and give feedback on these discussions to the group.

5. Groups should invite outside experts or qualified colleagues to attend the group meetings and should encourage them to challenge the group consensus.

6. Groups should appoint one member to be the official 'devil's advocate', to disagree with the consensus.

The consequences of distorted decisions have such a significant impact on service users that it is important take active measures to guard against distorted group thinking, whether or not service users are present during group deliberations.

Creating and sustaining an environment for continuous practice development

For effective analytical practice to be the norm – that is the baseline that it should be for service delivery – the teams and agencies in which they operate should support and encourage good analytical thinking and practice at every level. This involves creating and sustaining an agency culture that supports continuous development and reflection, both organisationally and on a practitioner and team level. This section will consider what can be done at the team and team manager level and at the organisational level to create a practice culture that supports analysis.

Agency culture

The leadership role is vital in encouraging critical thinking and reflection; and in giving permission for people to carve out the time they need to do so properly. The tone set within the agency in its priorities and approach to practice will permeate throughout the whole service, so it is important to deliberately cultivate the characteristics of agency culture covered in this section.

It is not enough for managers to talk about evidence-informed practice. Leaders of organisations and in turn their managers and staff need the 'raw materials' – including time and a valuing of 'thinking space' – to utilise evidence from a range of sources meaningfully. Workers should be encouraged to draw on theory and research, which involves providing them with the resources to do so easily and efficiently. Enabling evidence-based practice specifically is discussed in more detail later in this section.

Agencies also need to factor in and facilitate time for direct work with children, as a failure to adequately explore children's needs and experiences is often one of the most significant flaws in assessments.

An increased tendency towards 'managerialism' with components of practice measured and checked in mechanical ways can, if its limitations are not acknowledged, erode professionalism and autonomy and be insensitive at the case level. For example, an agency can place a high priority on fulfilling a Performance indicator relating to Looked after children reviews going ahead on time, but lose sight of the importance of enabling young people to participate in the review by implementing local rules – such as 'all review meetings *must* go ahead' even if the social worker is off sick, or the parent or child is sick – that can lead to a meeting that is of less value than it could have been.

There is clearly a need to collate information regarding whether standards are met, but efforts need to be made to ensure that practitioners do not think this is of a higher priority than service users' needs. It is more helpful to concentrate on how much time the worker spends with the child; in what range of settings; and what sense they have been able to make of what the child is communicating or experiencing; and to assist practitioners to achieve the analysis of information confidently and meaningfully.

The importance that senior managers appear to place on reflective practice should be demonstrated through their own actions and ways of doing things. For example, if leaders demonstrate open-mindedness; recognition that they can make mistakes and can always learn from them; and that getting at the truth is more important than winning an argument; then they are better placed to encourage this ethos throughout the whole organisation. If the agency culture is to expect workers to be decisive and strong in sticking to 'right' opinions once formed, it can be very difficult for workers to go back on their own thinking or be self-critical or to revise their conclusions – even though to be open to doing so is good practice. As Munro (2002, p.145) puts it, it can be tempting to 'close one's eyes and be uncritical'.

Finally, attention to analytic methods at the agency level helps guard against practice that is oppressive or unwittingly discriminating. The more explicit and clear we can be in our thinking, the more we can empower and involve service users.

Supervision

Perhaps one of the most direct influences on the ability of practitioners to work to optimum effectiveness is the quality of supervision available to them.

It is clear that both intuitive and analytical approaches have strengths and weaknesses. It was shown in Preparing for assessments (page 12) how a skilled practitioner will, at any one time, be drawing on a range of skills and methods along the continuum of intuition and analysis. It is therefore crucial that, in supervision, skills in intuition and empathy are nurtured and valued, while more objective mechanisms to aid analytical thinking are also encouraged.

Supervisors should prioritise the need for an overview or chronology, not as a paper exercise or because a court process requires it, but in order to provide rich information that may help a practitioner grow nearer to understanding how problems for a family came to be over time.

Supervisors can also support analysis by ensuring that a range of explanations for causes of concerns are explored over time, and by encouraging practitioners to seek to disconfirm their original hypotheses, actively hypothesising as described in Chapter 2 (page 24).

Practitioners should be enabled or challenged by supervisors to avoid being steered too readily into what can become a fairly entrenched 'agency view' in relation to families over time. This is particularly important with cases that have been known about over long periods of time. New workers to a case are often given an overview based on longstanding judgements. In particular if they lack confidence, experience or feel disempowered by the hierarchy, it is far easier to go along with this than to look anew at the family or child's circumstances and to challenge it. Tools such as the Critical Decision method (page 95) can be helpful to supervisors when assisting practitioners to learn from their own practice, as it uses a process that challenges the practitioner to really reflect on what they did and why. Klein (2000, p104) says experts learn and derive insights through accurate, diagnostic and timely feedback; and through reviewing past experiences. Supervisors are often well placed to provide such feedback.

What can teams do?

If an analytical approach to assessment work is to be embedded in a team's ethos and work, it is important that it is owned and responsibility is shared by all team members.

Teams should ensure that, as a group, they are fully aware of what existing structures and resources are in place to support them in their practice and development. These include local training, inter-agency forums, and PQ training opportunities; and organisations providing practitioners with opportunities to access information and web-based publications. Also, the use of existing tools such as the Questionnaires and Scales that accompany the *Framework for Assessment of Children in Need and their Families* (DH and others 2000) could be encouraged, if not already being utilised.

Many teams use their meeting time to go beyond the business of the team's day-to-day functions to spending time reflecting, learning or considering practice. Some of the tools in this toolkit could be used to focus that time on practice development sessions. With the many pressures social workers face, they might feel some resistance to the introduction of more formal analytic tools and to moving away from intuitive practice, particularly where 'tools' mean more forms to fill in. This is more likely if intuition and analysis are presented as polarised approaches in a way that fails to acknowledge the essential skills in empathy and intuition, without which practice would be ineffective and robotic.

If information officers are available to the team then they could seek out research evidence or literature reviews for practitioners on a given subject to assist their thinking in particular cases. However, where there is no such post, teams can support themselves by allocating designated areas of knowledge responsibility, to individual team members, for example someone signs up to specialist forums regarding domestic violence, someone else for asylum seeker issues and they then share their learning during team meetings, providing handouts or pointers to more detailed information where appropriate.

Developing a more evidence-based approach to practice at an organisational level

> Evidence-based decision-making requires not only a sound knowledge base regarding abuse and neglect but also an understanding of how the process of assessment can be undermined, and that steps that can be taken to protect against this.
>
> (Geraldine Macdonald, 2001 p.249)

As stated throughout this toolkit, improving the participant's analytic capacity involves actively trying to counter the natural tendencies for bias that undermine their practice, such as becoming attached to their early conclusions about families. As well as suggesting ways to identify when this is happening and tools to assist practitioners in their analysis of children's needs (as provided in this book), drawing on up-to-date research evidence is also an important part of enhancing the quality of assessments.

However, many practitioners are less clear than they would like to be about the content of research evidence, or how to access the information that will be most directly useful in their practice. To assist with this, we have provided a few examples of useful websites in the next section (Resources and useful information).

The sorts of 'evidence' referred to here are national and local research findings; good practice models; findings of service evaluations, including service-user feedback and data on short- and long-term outcomes for service users; inspection reports; and summaries of inspections.

If organisations are to truly promote and support evidence-based practice they need to consider drawing up a strategy to do so, appointing a steering group or lead person to oversee its implementation; and to draw up concrete action plans to bring about change.

Evidence-based practice should be a regular agenda item in meetings at every level and research evidence should be referred to in policy documents, and strategic plans.

User feedback should be sought, analysed and shared with staff along with any information that is available on short- and long-term outcomes for service users.

Resources such as specialist library access and information officers who can help others to find and make sense of information should be considered. Also, practitioners need easy access to the internet from or near their desks. Journals and books should be made readily available and learning from conferences and research events should be disseminated effectively within the organisation. Similar mechanisms for dissemination could be employed on a team level; with PQ students for example being given opportunities to share their learning with colleagues.

Supervision policies should stress that supporting evidence-based practice is a function of supervision. Development plans and appraisals of practitioners should pay attention to their needs in building on their practice in this area.

Finally, and perhaps the hardest to achieve, is that time for reflection and reading should be factored in when considering what individual practitioners and teams can achieve in terms of outputs.

References

Adcock, M (2000) 'The core assessment process: How to synthesise information and make judgements', in Horwath, J (ed) *The Child's World: Assessing children in need. The reader.* London: NSPCC.

Advisory Council on the Misuse of Drugs (2003) *Hidden Harm: Responding to the needs of children of problem drug users – The report of an inquiry by the Advisory Council on the misuse of drugs.* HMSO.

Anderson, T. (1990) *The Reflecting Team: Dialogues and Metadialogues.* Broadstairs: Borgmann.

Barnes, V and Chand, A (2001) 'Initial Assessments in Child Protection: The reality of practice', *Practice* 12, 4, 5–16.

Broad, B (2004) 'Kinship care for children in the UK: Messages from research, lessons for policy and practice', *European Journal of Social Work*, 7, 2, 211–28.

Broad, B, Hayes, R, and Rushforth, C (2001) *Kinship Care for Vulnerable Young People.* York: Joseph Rowntree Foundation.

Butler, I and Williamson, H (1994) *Children Speak: Children, trauma and social work.* Harlow: Longman.

Calder, Martin C and Hackett, S (eds) (2003) *Assessment in Childcare: Using and developing frameworks for practice.* Russell House Publishing.

Calder, Martin C, Harold, Gordon TMD and Howarth, Emma L (2004) *Children Living with Domestic Violence: Towards a framework for assessment.* Russell House.

Cash, S (2001) 'Risk assessment in child welfare: The art and science', *Children and Youth Services Review*, 23, 11, 811–30.

Caxton, G (1999) *Wise Up: The challenge of lifelong learning.* London: Bloomsbury.

Cleaver, H, Unel, I and Aldgate, A (1999) *Children's Needs – Parenting Capacity: The impact of parental mental illness, problem alcohol and drug use and domestic violence on children's development.* London: The Stationery Office.

Cleaver, H and Walker, S (2004a) *Assessing Children's Needs and Circumstances: The impact of the Assessment Framework.* London: Jessica Kingsley.

Cleaver, H and Walker, S (2004b) 'From policy to practice: The implementation of a new framework for social work assessments of children and families', *Child and Family Social Work*, 9, 81–90.

Department of Health (1995) *Child Protection: Messages from research.*

Department of Health and others (2000) *Framework for the Assessment of Children in Need and their Families: The family pack of questionnaires and scales.* London: The Stationery Office.

Department of Health and others (2002) *Safeguarding Children: The joint chief inspectors report on arrangements to safeguard children.* London: Department of Health.

Department of Health (2003) 12th Annual Report of the Chief Inspector of Social Services. London: HMSO.

Dreyfus, H and Dreyfus, S (1986) *Mind over Machine: The power of human intuition on expertise in the era of the computer.* New York: The Free Press.

Farmer, E and Owen, M (1995) *Child Protection Practice: Private risks and public remedies.* HMSO.

Forrester, D (2004) 'Social work assessments with parents who misuse drugs or alcohol' in Phillips, R *Children Exposed to Parental Substance Misuse: Implications for Family Placement* London: BAAF.

Hammond, R (1996) *Human Judgement and Social Policy*, Oxford University Press, cited in O'Sullivan, T (1999) *Decision-making in Social Work.* Palgrave.

Hart, D 'Assessment prior to birth', Ch. 15, in Horwath, J (ed)(2001) *The Child's World: Assessing children in need.* London: Jessica Kingsley.

Holland, S (2004) *Child and Family Assessment in Social Work Practice.* Sage Publications.

Hollows, A 'Making professional judgements in the framework for the assessment of children in need and their families, Ch. 3, in Calder, Martin C and Hackett, S (eds) (2003) *Assessment in Childcare: Using and developing frameworks for practice.* Russell House Publishing.

Horwath, J (ed) (2001) *The Child's World: Assessing children in need.* London: Jessica Kingsley.

Janis, I (1982) 'Groupthink: Psychological studies of policy decisions and fiascos', Boston, MA: Houghton Mifflin, cited in Munro, E (2002) *Effective Child Protection.* Sage Publications.

Jones, DPH, Hindley, P and Ramchandi, A 'Making plans, assessment, intervention and evaluating outcomes', in Aldgate, J and others (eds) (2006) *The Developing World of the Child.* Jessica Kingsley.

Klein, G (2000) *Sources of Power: How people make decisions.* Cambridge MA: MIT Press.

MacDonald, G (2001) *Effective Interventions for Child Abuse and Neglect: An evidence-based approach to planning and evaluating interventions.* Chichester: Wiley.

McCracken, DG (1988) *The Long Interview.* Beverly Hills, CA: Sage.

Miller, WR and Rollnick, S (2001) *Motivational interviewing: Preparing People for Change* 2nd ed. London: The Guilford Press.

Moon, J (1999) *Learning Journals: A handbook for academics, students and professional development.* London: Kogan Page.

Morgan, R (2005) *Getting the Best from Complaints: The children's view – what children and young people think about the government's proposals to change the social services complaints procedure.* Newcastle: Office of the Children's Rights Director.

Munro, E (1999) 'Common errors of reasoning in child protection work', *Child Abuse & Neglect*, 23, 8, 745–58.

Munro, E (2002) *Effective Child Protection.* Sage Publications.

NSPCC (1997*) Turning Points: A resource pack for communicating with children* (Module 2, Foundation Part of pack). NSPCC.

O'Sullivan, T (1999) *Decision-making in Social Work.* Basingstoke: Palgrave.

Phillips, R (ed) (2004) *Children Exposed to Parental Substance Misuse Implications for Family Placement.* BAAF.

Reder, P and Duncan, S (1999) *Lost Innocents: A follow-up study of fatal child abuse.* Routledge.

Schön, D A (1983) The Reflective Practitioner: How professionals think in action. New York: Basic Books.

Scott, D. (1998) 'A qualitative study of social work assessment in cases of alleged child abuse', *British Journal of Social Work*, 28 (1): 73–88

Seden, J and others (2001) *Studies Informing the Framework for the Assessment of Children in Need and their Families.* The Stationery Office.

Shaw, I (1997) *Be your Own Evaluator.* Wrexham: Prospects.

Sheldon, B (1987) 'The psychology of incompetence' in Blom-Cooper, L. (ed.), *After Beckford: Essays on Themes Connected with the Case of Jasmine Beckford.* London: Royal Holloway and Bedford New College.

Sheldon, B (2003) 'The risk of risks', *Evidence-based Social Care*, Autumn/Winter Issue, 15.

Sinclair, R (2001) referred to in Seden, J and others (2001) *Studies Informing the Framework for the Assessment of Children in Need and their Families.* The Stationery Office.

Tunnard, J (2002a) 'Parental drug misuse: A review of impact and intervention studies', *Research in Practice,* 2002.

Tunnard, J (2002b) 'Parental problem drinking and its impact on children', *Research in Practice,* 2002.

Tunnard, J (2004) 'Parental mental health problems messages from research policy and practice', *Research in Practice,* 2004.

Turnell, A and Edwards, S (1999) *Signs of Safety: A solution and safety orientated approach to child protection.* Norton and Co.

Wald, MS and Woolverton, M (1990*)* 'Risk Assessment: The emperor's new clothes', *Child Welfare,* 69, 483–551.

Williams, A and McCann, J (2006) *Care Planning for Looked After Children: Guidance and training materials for multi-agency working* [CD-Rom]. London: National Children's Bureau.

Winnicott, C (1977) 'Communicating with children' *Social Work Today,* 8, 26.

Resources and useful information

This section includes ideas and suggestions of where to access reliable up-to-date information, including research findings, theory, literature reviews, overviews and training materials.

Many organisations have undertaken reviews of what is known about subjects pertinent to social work, such as the impact of domestic violence, the needs of learning disabled parents, or the outcomes for looked after children in a range of areas. They distil the huge amount of information already available into manageable reviews, which they often evaluate and update over time. These provide invaluable resources to agencies and practitioners who need to draw on such information but do not have time to trawl through it all themselves.

Useful contacts

Research in Practice (RiP)

The RiP website (www.rip.org.uk) provides many resources to assist people in accessing research reviews, and evaluations of them, on a broad range of relevant subjects. It also has, along with many other useful functions, the EvidenceBank.

RiP has also developed, from their Change projects, the following tools for agencies and teams to draw on when working towards reviewing and improving their ability to support evidence-based practice.

■ *REAL* Organisational Support for Evidence-based Practice development project.

■ TEAMWISE: Using research and evidence. The handbook produced from this project can be ordered from the website and has 21 tools in it to assist teams in developing practice.

Further information on these can be accessed from the RiP website (above).

Making Research Count

This is a national collaborative research dissemination initiative, currently run by ten regional centres based in the Universities of East Anglia; Brighton; Keele; Luton; King's College, London; Nottingham; Salford; The Open University; Warwick; and York. This consortium of universities has a proven track record in social work and social care research, as well as providing social work education at qualifying and post-qualifying levels. These ten universities work in partnership with over sixty local authorities, NHS Trusts and other agencies, with a view to:

■ promoting knowledge-based, research-informed practice

■ improving the dissemination of research

■ strengthening the research-mindedness and critical appraisal skills of social work and social care practitioners.

The Making Research Count website can be accessed at: http://www.uea.ac.uk/swk/MRC_web/public_html/

The Oxford Centre for Research into Parenting and Children

This multi-disciplinary centre brings together researchers in the University of Oxford, as well as researchers nationally and internationally with whom they have worked, who are researching into issues relating to parenting and children.

The aims of the centre are:

- to develop a better understanding of the well-being of parents and children; what causes problems (health, educational and social); and how they may be ameliorated
- to build multi-disciplinary, national and international research links
- to act as a discussion forum for researchers from different disciplines and for practitioners (health, education and social) who work with children and families
- to disseminate research findings.

The centre website contains links to the work of a number of researchers, including Dr Ann Buchanan who is the centre director, Dr David Jones and Kathy Sylva. www.apsoc.ox.ac.uk/parenting

Social Care Institute of Excellence

The is another useful source of information, running specific networks such as the Parental Mental Health and Child Welfare Network, conducting knowledge reviews (so called because they often include not only literature overviews, but views and input from practitioners and users as well) and a website with a number of useful links and functions. www.scie.org.uk

Membership organisations

Membership organisations, such as the following, also provide information and summaries of topics in various forms.

National Children's Bureau (NCB), at www.ncb.org.uk publish a series of research summaries in *Highlights,* available from NCB Online Bookshop, www.ncb-books.org.uk

Parenting UK, at www.parentinguk.org has information aimed at professionals who work with parents, including publications and briefings.

Barnardo's, at www.barnardos.org.uk has research and publications available to purchase or download, including the *What Works* series.

National Society for the Prevention of Cruelty to Children (NSPCC), at www.nspcc.org.uk has publications, information, leaflets, links and research studies available, including the NSPCC Inform service.

Drugscope, at www.drugscope.org.uk provides a library and information service; and has journals, and directories of information about drugs and of services.

Office of the United Nation's High Commissioner for Human Rights, at www.ohchr.org provides information about human rights issues including children's rights under the UN Convention as well as access to relevant links and publications.

Contact a Family, at www.contactafamily.org.uk is a UK-wide charity providing support, advice and information for families with disabled children. They also operate a helpline on 0808 808 3555 on Mondays from 10–4 and 5–7 and from Tuesday–Fridays between 10am and 4pm

National Association for the Care and Resettlement of Offenders at www.nacro.org.uk is a crime reduction charity. The website contains information about their services in addition to information leaflets, briefings and publications about aspects of working with offenders, for example Looked After young people who offend or people with mental health problems.

The National Institute of Mental Health in England (NIMHE), at www.nimhe.org.uk, lists publication and resources; provides links, for example, to the Mental Health Research Network; and provides articles on current plans and activities.

Joseph Rowntree Foundation, at www.jrf.org.uk, provides a bookshop and findings from research projects.

Library and Information services can be accessed including text access to journals at: www.swetswise.com/direct.do

and at the British Library Inside service at www.inside.bl/user/secure/logon/do

Government websites

These websites provide access to guidance, publications and policy documents.

Department of Health – www.dh.gov.uk

Department for Education and Skills – www.dfes.gov.uk

www.everychildmatters.gov.uk – a separate website that provides information on every aspect of the current change agenda for children's services, including information on the aims of the Every Child Matters programme, outcomes for children, strategy and delivering services. The site contains case studies and links to other resources.

Social Exclusion Unit – www.socialexclusion.gov.uk

Home Office – www.homeoffice.gov.uk

Local Government Information Unit – www.lgiu.gov.uk

Office for National Statistics – www.statistics.gov.uk

Sure Start – www.surestart.gov.uk

Further reading

Burton, Sheryl (1997) *When There's A Will There's A Way: Refocusing child care practice – A guide for team managers.* NCB.

Chaffin, M and others (1997) 'The abuse dimensions inventory: Initial data on a research measure of abuse severity', *Journal of Interpersonal Violence,* 12, 4, August, 569–89.

City of Salford Community and Social Services (2000) *Conducting Family Assessments: A practice guide.* Russell House Publishing.

Directors of Social Work in Scotland (1992) *Child Protection: Policy, practice and procedure.* Edinburgh: HMSO.

Dowie, J and Elstein, A (1998) *Professional Judgement: A reader in clinical decision-making.* Cambridge University Press.

Dufour, S and Chamberland, C (2004) 'The effectiveness of selected interventions for previous maltreatment: Enhancing the well-being of children who live at home', *Child & Family Social Work*, 9, 39–56.

Fenman Ltd (2003) 'The definitive guide to creating a great learning experience', *Train the Trainer,* 1–25, 2003–2005.

Flynn, R (2000) 'Kinship foster care', *Highlight,* 179.

Gigerenzer, G and others (1999) *Simple Heuristics that Make us Smart.* Oxford University Press, 3–33.

Gopfert, Webster J and Seeman, Mary V (eds) (2004) *Parental Psychiatric Disorder: Distressed parents and their families.* Cambridge University Press.

Gorin, S (2004) *Understanding What Children Say: Children's experiences of domestic violence, parental substance misuse and parental health problems.* NCB.

Henniker, J, Print, B and Morrison, T (2002) An inter-agency assessment framework for young people who sexually abuse: Principles, processes and practicalities. *Child Care in Practice*, 8, 2.

Holt, R, Grundon, J and Paxton, R (1998) 'Specialist assessment in child protection proceedings: Problems and possible solutions', *Child Abuse Review*, 7, 266–79.

Jack, G, and Gill, O (2003) *The Missing Side of the Triangle: Analysing the influence of wider family and environmental factors on parenting and child development.* Barkingside: Barnardo's.

Kearney, P, Levin, E, and Rosen, G (2003) *Alcohol, drug and mental health problems: Working with Families.* SCIE.

Madge, N (2001) *Understanding Difference: The meaning of ethnicity for young lives.* NCB.

Madge, N and others (2000) *The Forgotten Years*: 9–13. NCB.

Newman, T and Blackburn, S (2002) *Interchange 78: Transitions in the Lives of Children and Young People – Resilience Factors.* Scottish Executive Education Dept.

Randall, J, Cowley, P and Tomlinson, P (2000) 'Overcoming barriers to effective practice in child care. *Child and Family Social Work*, 5, 343–52.

Reder, P and Lucey, R (eds) (1995) *Assessment of Parenting: Psychiatric and psychological contributions.* Routledge.

Reder, P, Duncan, S, and Lucey, C (eds) (2003) *Studies in the Assessment of Parenting.* Brunner-Routledge.

van Nijnatten, C, van den Ackerveken, M and Ewals, T (2004) 'Managing assessment quality planning in assessment procedures of the Dutch Child Protection Board', *British Journal of Social Work*, 34, 531–40.

Ward, H and Rose, W (eds)(2002) *Approaches to Needs Assessment in Children's Services.* London: Jessica Kingsley.

Walker, S (2003) *Social Work and Child and Adolescent Mental Health.* Russell House Publishers.

Webb, S (2001) 'Some considerations on the validity of evidence-based practice in social work', *British Journal of Social Work*, 31, 57–79.

Appendix

Presentations

The presentations below are available in PowerPoint and PDF formats. They can be downloaded from www.ncb.org.uk/resources/support. The presentations can be used in team-development or training courses.

Presentation 1: Analysis, intuition and the nature of expertise

1

Effective child protection
Eileen Munro

- Intuitive/analytical debate in social work
- Strengths/weaknesses of both approaches
- Understanding of decision theory and its usefulness to social work
- Context of influences on development of body of social work theory
- Introduction of model – Decision trees
- Application to practice

2

Analytical–Intuitive

Analytical
- Formal logic
- Probability theory
- Decision theory
- Formal instruments
- Empirical research
- Measure specific dimensions
- Statistical equations

Intuitive
- How people reason
- Establishing rapport
- Using empathy and experience
- Imagination
- Unconscious appraisal of competence

3

Intuition
strengths–weaknesses

Strengths
- Fundamental
- Swift
- Interpersonal
- Draws on knowledge and research
- Tacit – even if can't be articulated, still valuable
- Survived over time

Weaknesses
- Implicit – defective as shared public knowledge
- Not necessarily reliable
- Limited to range of own experience and bias
- Blind spots – look for evidence to confirm assumptions
- Doesn't acknowledge variables

4

Analytical reasoning
strengths–weaknesses

Strengths
- Knowledge base from empirical research – a lot done
- Summaries and critiques readily available
- All aspects of subject have been studied
- Need to justify actions – public accountability

Weaknesses
- Findings tentative – only weak causal link at times
- Can't just read findings – need to understand context, use judgement
- Difficult to export to different populations
- Definitions of child abuse change over time
- Can't have random control trials in child protection studies (unethical)

5

However...

- Actuarial tools
  - do demonstrate a higher level of accuracy and consistency than professional judgements
  - provide opportunity for consistency across agency and workers
  - can play a part in overall case management
  - help in developing clear standards
  - are not infallible

6

Messages for social work

- Social workers need to become more analytical and critical to improve accuracy
- Empathy and intuition central – but practice can be improved by developing analytical skills
- Formal methods don't offer certainty. SWs should be cautious about the level of accuracy they can hope to achieve
- Child abuse is a phenomenon shaped by social context

7

Categories of skills

- Formal knowledge
- Reasoning skills
- Practice wisdom
- Values
- Emotional wisdom

8

Activity

- Choose a case that you are involved with or is familiar to you
- Plot a pathway through different points at which decisions were made (big and small)
- Can you identify categories of knowledge and skills you applied at each point?
- Would this be different depending on your length of practice experience ?

9

Evidence-based practice
Simon Hackett, University of Durham

- Widespread support for the notion that social workers should ground their work in empirical evidence
- Few would disagree that account should be taken of research findings
- Few would wish to defend practice approaches that have no apparent effect
- Growing support for transparent practice

10

Evidence-based practice
the pitfalls

- Difficulty applying research to practice
- Always a dichotomy in research findings
- Politics of research
- Financial constraints
- Confidence in applying research
- Lack of expertise/knowledge
- Dealing with individuals – too many variables

11

Evidence-based practice
the benefits

- Encourages reflective practice
- Improves outcomes for children
- Targets resources
- Increases professionalism
- Clarifies and informs thinking
- Leads to new approaches or confirms existing ones
- Enhances practice and confidence

12

Common errors of reasoning in child protection

Eileen Munro

- Failure to revise risk assessments – difficulty in changing minds, considering alternative perspectives
- Failure to look at own files, past information overlooked
- Failure to take a long-term perspective, to note emerging patterns
- Written evidence overlooked in preference to direct reports

13

Common errors of reasoning

- Scepticism about new evidence that challenges existing views
- Uncritical about evidence that supports existing view
- Parents' reactions during assessment taken as representative
- Failure to check 'facts' and information
- Tendency to 'groupthink' – conformity

14

Decision theory

- Sets out framework for considering possible options, considering the consequences, how probable they are, judging how good or bad those outcomes would be and picking the option that you believe will have the most beneficial consequences

15

Decision tree activity

- Form groups of 5 or 6
- Using the case study, construct a decision tree identifying the possible options for interventions
- Identify possible consequences of each course of action, pros and cons of each consequence
- Score different options
- Give feedback on main issues

Presentation 2: Analysing, hypothesising and reporting

1

Analysing and reporting
Sally Holland

Holland S (2004) *Child and Family Assessment in Social Work*, Sage.

2

The process of analysis in assessment

- Analysis pervades assessment from beginning
- Social research – a solid foundation for analysing info
- Difficulties in articulating thinking
- Process provides clarity for self and others

3

Analysis in assessment and social research

- Tendency to be verificationists – confirming original explanations
- Need to do more than aim to be neutral – counter this tendency
- Processes used to analyse data in qualitative research may be useful

4

Ways of analysing qualitative research

- **Analytic induction** Data is examined and hypotheses/explanations are developed and examined against data. Contradictory data means theory is abandoned or modified. Process continues with hypotheses being discarded and refined.
- **Deductive processes** Begin with hypothesis and examine data in the light of these.
- **Retroduction** Synthesis of both. Drawn from data and tests data against existing concepts.

5

Parallel with family work

- Look for info that will test potential ways of understanding and helping
- Also be open to new ways of understanding and helping that are rooted in the info that is emerging
- Always look for data that might disprove or throw doubt on our understanding

6

Reflexivity

- Process where we are critically aware of the impact of ourselves and our belief systems on the assessment and the service-users' response to this
- Includes, gender, race, professional status, agency culture dominant theories
- Cultural review (EXERCISE)

7

Building hypothesis

- Hypothesis is a testable proposition
- Understanding the family situation and the best way forward
- How difficulties are experienced (particularly by child)
- May include antecedents

8

Building hypothesis
the process

- Progressive hypothesis development
  – one at a time
- Comparative hypothesis development
  – all at same time
- Attention to assessment methods
  – interviewing
  – observing
  – questionnaires

9

The process

- Actively seek evidence to disconfirm or challenge hypothesis – avoid simply confirming the dominant concern
- Managing the data:
  – notes in margins
  – highlighting themes (coding)
  – analyse info from various sources
  – key words
- Be conscious of value placed on sources of hypothesis

10

Sources of hypothesis

- Service-user explanations – listen and take seriously
- Practitioners explanation, practice wisdom
- Evidence-based practice, wide reading of research
- Theory, having and using ideas

11

Sharing explanations

- Constantly check out views with others
- Supervision critical
- Consultations with other agencies
- Avoid groupthink
- Share with those being assessed

12

Reaching conclusions

- Reaching saturation point – drawing conclusions
- Never going to be indisputable
- Conclusions that look forward rather than back (solution-focused)
- Flexible to changing circumstances

13

Reporting the assessment

- Organisational culture is inherent in reporting style
- Forms not neutral
- Considering the audience (who might the audience be?)
- Service-user access

14

Reporting

- Balance
- Views of service-users
- Decision-making process
- Language use
- Ordering of points – prioritisation

Presentation 3: Needs–led assessment

1

Needs-led assessment

Aim

To revise/refocus on needs-led planning for children

2

Needs-led assessment

Objectives

By the end of the session, participants will have:

- had an overview of a needs-led approach in relation to individual and service planning
- have identified challenges in practice in staying needs-led
- have practised needs-led identification
- have used needs-led assessment in a planning process

3

Why needs led?

- Inspection reports have found it is not always clear how the services provided meet the needs of children (e.g. Hounslow)
- Variation, since Children Act, about how LAs interpret and meet need (dominance of child protection)
- Tendency towards deterrent prevention (Aldgate 2001)
- Haphazard pattern of access to services with little matching of needs and services, 'sticking-plaster approach' (Children Act overview)

4

Benefits of needs-led approach

- Helps children and their parents and workers understand what must be done and what needs to change in order to meet needs (partnership)
- Fairness of access and transparency
- Useful in family placement assessments
- Useful in service planning as well as individual work

5

Activity 1

- In pairs or groups of three, look at the case study you have been given
- Identify this child's needs under each dimension and write each need on a separate sticky note
- After 10 minutes, come and put sticky notes up under the child's name and specific dimensions on the list

Presentation 4: Signs of safety approach

1

Signs of safety approach

- Background and origins
- Underpinning philosophy
- Practice principles for partnership
- Six practice elements
- Interactive exercise

2

Background and origins

- Andrew Turnell and Steve Edwards
- Early 1990s: Parent-teen link programme, Perth Western Australia (Brief Therapy Intervention)
- Collaboration with Berg and Shazer: Founders of Solution-focused Brief Therapy (Wisconsin)
- Collaboration with Child Protection colleagues
- Could Brief Therapy be used in Child Protection settings?

3

Aims
(Turnell and Edwards)

- To increase confidence of child protection workers in their own practice
- To enable them to more readily make and commit to judgements based on a balance of information regarding danger and safety
- To develop an approach that was focused on solution and safety, and field tested by social workers

4

Aims
Practitioners

To identify an approach that:
- Would get them unstuck in difficult and protracted cases
- Was flexible and responsive to diverse client situations
- Was applicable from intake through to case closure
- Drew on clients' strengths whilst being mindful of safety of children

5

Programme

- Literature search on customer perspectives in Child Protection
- Training on brief solution-focused therapy
- Development of format for assessment, including forms
- Handbook for practitioners

6

Programme

- Management of change issues learnt from first attempt to deliver programme
- Important to assume considerable experience and good practice of workers they are training
- Case examples from fellow workers most helpful
- Have continued to develop approach over last 12 years in collaboration with child care SW colleagues

7

Practice principles

- Respect service recipients as people worth doing business with
- Cooperate with the person not the abuse
- Recognise that cooperation is possible even where coercion is required
- Recognise that all families have signs of safety
- Maintain a focus on safety

8

Principles (cont)

- Learn what the recipient wants
- Always search for detail
- Focus on creating small change
- Don't confuse case details with judgements
- Offer choices
- Treat the interview as a forum for change

9

Six practice elements

- Understand the position of each family member
- Find exceptions to the maltreatment
- Discover family strengths and resources
- Focus on goals
- Scale safety and progress
- Assess willingness, confidence and capacity

10

Group exercise

- In your groups take the practice element you have been ascribed
- Plan and deliver a 5–7 minute presentation describing this element to your colleagues
- Give one example of where a group member has used such an approach in practice (or could do so)

Presentation 5: Involving children

1

Involving children – the background

- Children Act 1989 – ascertainable wishes and feelings
- UN Convention on the Rights of the Child, articles:
  2 (equality), 3 (best interests), 6 (right to survival and development), 12 (right to express views freely), 4 (those views to be respected).
- Against a background of changing conceptions of childhood/children's rights over time

2

Basics

- Knowing the child
- Building trust
- Self awareness of worker and boundaries
- Choice and empowerment
- Environment/context
- Including the family
- Child observation/play
- Support

3

Involving children in assessments

References:

Sally Holland (2004) *Child and Family Assessment in Social Work Practice*, Chapter 6, Sage.

Ian Butler and Howard Williamson (1994) *Children Speak: Children, trauma and social work*, NSPCC, Longman.

4

What children have told us they do and don't want

Don't want
- A 'robotic', procedure led approach
- Fixed views
- Not listening
- 'Spreading things'
- Abandoning

Do want
- Listening
- Availability
- Non-judgemental/non-directive
- Humour & quirks
- Honesty/straight talking
- Trust/confidentiality

5

Coastal cities study
Sally Holland

- Though SWs used child-centred language, children were 'minor characters' in the narrative
- Two-dimensional descriptions of children, mainly based on their responses to parents
- Children often described with 'detached objectivity' (Sheridan chart language)

6

Coastal cities study (cont.)

- In some cases, children's views were prominent but the weight given to them variable
- Social workers were ambivalent about the worth of obtaining children's opinions

7

Examples from Coastal cities study: Child's views

- "Elizabeth presents as whimsical and materialistic and may not be impressed by the current accommodation … It is clear that Elizabeth has changed her mind on a number of occasions"

8

Examples from Coastal cities study (cont.)

"Paul has remained consistent in his expressed wish to have Mr Taylor return home … Paul presents as a very sensible child who I feel would not hesitate to voice any feelings of unease"

9

Child development

- Children often described in relation to their progress against 'developmental norms'
- Critics of 'developmental dominance' argue that the theories tend to be prescriptive and universal in their assumptions (Burman 1994)

10

Attachment theory

- As with all theories, need to be critical and thoughtful in our application. Powerful arguments could be made by using a flawed or overly narrow evidence base
- Aspects of the theories criticised due to their origins, contradictions and applications

11

Attachment theory (cont.)

- All reports referred either directly or indirectly to attachment
- However, whilst important points were made, often only a partial aspect of the child's attachment behaviour was observed, which in contact tends to be emotionally charged and 'artificial'

12

Ways in which children's voices are silenced

- By not reporting the child's voice when recounting their experiences
- By objectifying through use of emphasis and language
- Presupposing what the child might say
- Presenting their voices as subjective, biased and untrustworthy

13

Summary of suggestions for practice

- Child should have access to clear information about the assessment process and its implications
- Consult children about assessment methods
- Children's preferences for expressing themselves verbally, through play, art and writing to be explored and harnessed. (Focus on what child *can* do and not what they can't)

14

Suggestions for practice (cont.)

- Allow for relationship-building in order to become familiar with a child's individuality
- Children say they are looking for honesty, reliability and confidentiality
- When portraying children's lives give a holistic picture
- All above applies equally to children of all abilities including disabled children
- Focus on 'meanings' for the child

Presentation 6: Assessing the impact of parental substance abuse on childcare

1

Assessing the Impact of Parental Substance Misuse on Childcare

2

Summary

- Definitions and prevalence
- Patterns and values
- Risk factors
- Impact on children
- Promoting good outcomes

3

When does 'use' become 'misuse'?

Dependency

'A compulsion or desire to continue taking a drug ... in order to feel good or avoid feeling bad'
(SCODA 1997)

4

Advisory Council on the Misuse of Drugs problem drug use

'That with serious negative consequences of a physical, psychological, social and interpersonal, financial or legal nature for users and those around them'

5

Prevalence

- 250,000–350,000 children in UK
- Less than half of drug-addicted parents in the UK live with their children
- Advisory Council on the Misuse of Drugs (2003)

6

Prevalence (cont.)

- One in three families referred to social services for concerns about child protection have recorded substance misuse or mental health issues.
(Falkov 1998)

7

Prevalence: Alcohol

'Approximately one million children in UK living with parental alcohol misuse.'
Childline (1997) 'Beyond the Limit'

8

Donald Forrester

- Raises importance of critical awareness of values so as to avoid distortion of assessment – unfair stereotypes or failing to see risk
- Focus on actual or likely effect on child. What are they at risk of?

9

Risk factors

- Presence of young babies
- Families where high levels of violence/alcohol
- Dual diagnosis
- Inadequate storage
- Daily heroin use
- Daily alcohol use/illicit drugs
- Regular stimulant use
- Sharing injecting equipment

10

Social risk factors

- Unstable accommodation
- Living alone or with strangers
- Living with another drug user
- Criminal justice involvement

(SCODA guidelines help us consider impact on parenting)

11

Implications for parenting capacity

Need to consider:
- Pattern of use
- How drugs are procured
- Health risks
- Parents' perception of situation

12

Family and environmental factors

- Physical needs/home environment
- Social networks and support
- Interconnected problems

13

Impact on children: Coping mechanisms

- Responsibility
- Avoidance
- Acting out
- (Consider different age groups)

14

Children's development

- Neonatal abstinence syndrome
- Viruses/health risks
- Chaotic use/supervision & care
- Motor/cognitive/behavioural – lack of consistency and 'negative command'
- Pre-school/school attendance and progress

15

Children's development (cont.)

- Normalisation of crime/deceit and secrecy
- Exposure to aggression/violence
- Restricted friendships/isolation
- Behavioural/emotional disturbance heightened during puberty
- 15+ greater risk of using substances, early sexual activity and lower educational attainment

16

Protective factors

- Another caring adult
- Financial resources
- Good standards in home conditions
- Alternative safe residence
- Help from health and social services
- Regular school attendance
- One good friend
- Trusted adults
- Further ed/job

17

Forrester, D (2004)

- Limited evidence that children's difficulties persist into adulthood
- Velleman and Orford: Links in a chain
- Parental denial/minimisation (motivational interviewing) (Miller and Rollnick 2001)

18

Forrester: Four assessment principles

- Maintain focus on child
- See adults' ability to manage own life as an indicator
- Past behaviour (chronology, involving parent)
- Use varied/wide sources

19

Promoting good outcomes

- Building on protective factors
- Communicating with child/young person
- Identifying supportive 'others'
- Partnership approach (with family)
- Effective inter-agency partnerships
- Making use of local family support resources

Presentation 7: Putting Analysis into Assessment

1

Putting Analysis into Assessment

Putting Analysis into Assessment
Project 2003–2005

Ruth Dalzell and Emma Sawyer
Family Support Unit
National Children's Bureau

2

Aim

To increase practitioner skills and confidence in analysis and judgement within assessment practice with children in need

3

Objectives

- To explore the policy and practice context of decision-making and judgement
- To provide an opportunity to assess strengths and weaknesses in use of analysis in assessment
- To introduce models and approaches which will strengthen assessment practice with children in need

4

Objectives [cont]

- To test out the application of approaches to complex situations and consider how these can help in making and reporting judgements within assessments
- To highlight relevant research and theory and share positive practice

5

Putting analysis into assessment

- Context
- Why important
- Assessment framework
- NCB Project
- Key themes emerging

6

Context in Children's Services

- Reforming Govt
- Modernising Local Govt, Performance Assessment Framework
- Improvement Agenda:Quality Protects Performance indicators
- Assessment framework
- Every Child Matters/Children Bill
- Integrating services and inspection
- Common assessment framework

7

Why concern about analysis?

- Evidence that Assessment framework has improved practice but:
- Research and Inspections have highlighted that analysis and professional judgement are the areas of assessment that continue to cause concern
- Analysis not given a great deal of attention in the assessment framework or the literature accompanying it

8

Inspections

- Managers and practitioners must ensure that the experience of the child is central to their analysis of facts
- Assessment reports reflected concerted efforts to collect information but far less evidence of analysis and evaluation

9

Assessment framework

Introduced to:
- Standardise assessment practice across England
- Increase child focus in assessments
- Ensure that assessment determined plan for child and were focused on
  - developmental needs
  - parental capacity
  - context of family and wider environment

10

Core theories underpinning framework

- Human needs
- Developmental theories
- Attachment theory
- Resilience theory
- Ecological perspective
- Theories of parental capacity

11

What are the strengths?

- Provides common framework which has been widely accepted (The triangle)
- Soundly based in theory and research
- Provides a holistic view of children's needs

12

What are the weaknesses?

- Accompanying guidance isn't widely used and, therefore, there is a reliance on the forms, which may produce fragmented view
- Doesn't encourage analysis – blank form, little guidance
- Questionnaires and scales – not adopted widely

13

Putting analysis into assessment project

To improve assessment in childcare practice by working with social work practitioners and managers to:
- Explore how professional confidence, knowledge and skills relating to analysis and judgement in assessment might be improved

14

Methods

- Working in depth with two Local Authorities
- Wider dissemination
- Providing opportunities for practitioners to examine how they make judgements

15

Practice development activities

- Theories of decision-making
- Needs-led assessment
- Signs of Safety
- Involving children
- Undertaking assessments with substance misusing families
- Using social research

16

Key themes

- Thorough assessments – compliant with procedures on the whole
- Lack of reference to research and theory in assessment reports
- Tendency to see core assessments as internal working tool
- Some practitioner's view that assessment forms don't generally lead towards analysis.

17

Key themes [cont]

- Resistance to starting assessments (ticking clock)
- Lack of standardisation about length/detail in assessments
- 'Workings out' not shown in assessments
- Children not very visible in assessments – lack of creativity
- More partnership with – focus on adult needs